A GRAND STRATEGY FOR THE WEST

Henry L. Stimson Lectures
Yale University

Helmut Schmidt

A Grand Strategy for the West

The Anachronism of National Strategies in an Interdependent World

Introduction by William P. Bundy

YALE UNIVERSITY PRESS   NEW HAVEN AND LONDON

Designed by Sally Harris
and set in Trump Medieval type by
Rainsford Type, Ridgefield, Connecticut.
Printed in the United States of America by
Vail Ballou Press, Binghamton, New York.

Library of Congress Card Catalog Number: 85–51657
International Standard Book Number: 0–300–03535–7

The paper in this book meets the guidelines for
permanence and durability of the Committee on
Production Guidelines for Book Longevity of the
Council on Library Resources.

10 9 8 7 6 5 4 3 2

Contents

Foreword
William J. Foltz

This book presents to a wider audience the Stimson Lectures that Helmut Schmidt delivered in the spring of 1985 at Yale University. The Yale Center for International and Area Studies has in the past brought distinguished scholars and men in public life to the Yale campus as Stimson Lecturers, but none has generated as much enthusiastic and sustained attention as the former Chancellor of the Federal Republic of Germany. The attention, which twice forced changes in venue to find a hall capable of holding the audience, stemmed in part from Helmut Schmidt's international renown. What sustained it, however, were the frankness, intensity, and intellectual weight of the arguments presented by a man who himself has turned thoughts into public policy and who knows at first hand the consequences that selfish and ill-considered thought may have when backed by the power of modern nations.

Speeches and books by retired statesmen risk disappointing serious audiences in two ways. The first, to which American politicians particularly seem prone, is the *post hoc* justification, buttressed by selective memory, of the author's past policies and intentions. The second, more a European temptation, is the visionary philosophical statement in which the author seems freed not only from the burdens of office, but from respect for the ordinary constraints of international reality and the intractabilities of human nature. Justification and vision are not absent from Helmut Schmidt's arguments, but both are subjected to the harsh discipline of reality, bluntly and logically confronted.

The Henry L. Stimson Fund for Research in World Affairs, which supported these lectures, bears the following indenture: "The purpose of this fund shall be the furtherance of basic research in all fields of learning and endeavor significant to world peace and to all fundamental human problems underlying the causes of war." The Fund honors a remarkable public servant and a remarkable person who, one ventures to guess, would have been pleased that Helmut Schmidt gave these lectures bearing his name. Many of Stimson's personal traits, thoughts, and public responsibilities parallel those of the former German Chancellor, born just a half century later. A "New England conscience on legs," Stimson was not shy about making his opinions known, whatever the consequences for his personal relations or public fortunes. Stimson was a "doer" who wished above all to be judged by his actions. He served his country most notably as Secretary of War 1911–13, Secretary of State 1929–33, and again Secretary of War from 1940 to the end of World War II. In and out of public office Stimson was an advocate of what we would now call deterrence based on military preparedness. He was a staunch believer that the United States had to assume special responsibilities to stabilize the international economic system. He was an advocate of a generous peace to build and safeguard a stable world order. In his last act as Secretary of War, Stimson wrote the first proposal for international agreements to control nuclear weapons. These very themes, as current issues, underlie Helmut Schmidt's 1985 Stimson Lectures.

The original lectures have been revised by Chancellor Schmidt for presentation in book form and to take into account points raised spontaneously in the long and lively question and answer sessions. William P. Bundy generously provided expert and helpful editorial suggestions. Chapter 6 includes additional material from Helmut Schmidt's article in *Die Zeit* of May 3, 1985.

Introduction   *William P. Bundy*

The troubled and frustration-laden period of the 1970s
and early 1980s has produced few statesmen of mem-
orable or heroic stature, either within individual nations or at the international level. It is my personal
view that the single individual most deserving that
label is the author of this volume, Helmut Schmidt,
Chancellor of the Federal Republic of Germany from
the spring of 1974 to the early fall of 1982.

During those years West Germany moved from
being, as many have put it, an economic giant but a
political dwarf to a political role commensurate with
its pivotal geographic position, economic standing,
and internal stability. More than to any other single
factor, this was due to Schmidt's leadership in dealing with a succession of critical security and economic problems for his country, for the Western
alliance, and for the wider world.

—A long-time staunch supporter of NATO, and
of the integration of West Germany into the
framework of Western cooperation, he took the
lead in the 1970s, when America was reeling
from the impact of the Vietnam War, in enlarg-
ing the European role in conventional defense
and deterrence. First as Defense Minister and
then as Chancellor, he did more than anyone
else to build the contemporary German armed
forces into an effective defensive force, with
strong reserves for any crisis, but at the same

time a force that could not fairly be seen to threaten any type of offensive action;

—At the same time, in keeping with NATO's agreed long-term strategy of defense *and* dialogue (accepted in the Harmel Report of 1967), he supported and then carried forward the Ostpolitik of his predecessor, Willy Brandt, opening up new ties to East Germany and to the countries of Eastern Europe, including trade with the Soviet Union itself;

—As the first oil shock of 1973–74 ignited the smoldering fires of inflation and set off a deep recession, Schmidt's direction of the German economy, as Economic and Finance Minister and then as Chancellor, was a model of steadiness, by common consent more effective than that of any other Western country save perhaps Japan;

—Then, as volatile exchange rates slowed lasting recovery, and in the face of what he saw as inadequate fiscal and monetary policies by the natural leader of the alliance—the United States—Schmidt combined in 1979 with his French counterpart (who became also his close friend), President Valéry Giscard d'Estaing, to pioneer the European Monetary System—which has since then at least cushioned the impact of currency fluctuations for most of Western Europe;

—In the Western economic summit meetings that began in 1975, Schmidt was an outstanding

participant, not always in step with the wishes
of successive U.S. administrations but always
forcing harder looks at key issues of energy and
economic policy;
—In 1976–78, when mindless terrorists targeted
especially the Federal Republic, Schmidt han-
dled a succession of harrowing crises with great
courage and wisdom, proving to his countrymen
and the world that Germans today could deal
with such threats without impairing their democratic values or practices.

In each of these areas of policy, the institutions
and approaches for which Schmidt was largely responsible have today become embedded and generally approved. Yet at the time each was intensely
controversial. That he was able to accomplish so
much was due in part to a depth of experience any
American President might envy—in handling crises
in Hamburg, then as a parliamentary expert on trans-
portation and defense, rising to become in 1967 parliamentary leader of the Social Democratic Party in
the Bundestag, and then successively as Defense
Minister and Economic and Finance Minister under
Brandt.* It also reflected tireless work and effective
and candid advocacy to both public and parliament.

*Jonathan Carr, *Helmut Schmidt: Helmsman of Germany* (New York:
St. Martin's, 1985), is an excellent and objective biography by a British
journalist. For American readers, Carr's book may be particularly useful
on Schmidt's early life, including his military service on the Western
and Eastern fronts and then as a staff officer in the Air Ministry in
Berlin.

In some areas of policy, especially in his later years as Chancellor, Schmidt met with disappointments and misunderstandings. Whereas his relationship with President Gerald Ford had been extraordinarily close and warm, he was never able to work easily or frankly with Jimmy Carter or Ronald Reagan, and the resulting strains were an added burden on one who always drove himself and his colleagues to the limit.

Thus, in those latter years, Schmidt had to deal with:

—the 1978 fiasco of the "neutron bomb," abandoned by Carter after Schmidt in particular had been reluctantly persuaded to accept it;
—the deployment of new U.S. intermediate-range nuclear missiles in Europe in response to the Soviet SS-20 threat. Foremost at the outset in calling for a firm and specific NATO response, Schmidt came to have misgivings about U.S. handling of the INF negotiations, and in the summer of 1982 neither he nor any other European leader was consulted when President Reagan made a major decision to sidetrack U.S. negotiator Paul Nitze's compromise proposal (the so-called "walk in the woods" formula);
—the frustration, through the defeat of Giscard d'Estaing in the French elections of 1981, of the unique and promising Franco-German relationship he and Giscard had forged and were about

to expand into new military and technological links. As Schmidt saw it, extraordinarily close ties between these two past enemies—not at the expense of either's relationship with the United States—had (and still have) the potential, as perhaps nothing else, of transforming the role of Western Europe in NATO and making it a genuine twin pillar, with North America, of the alliance;

—and the economic consequences of the second oil shock of 1979–80, after the Iranian Revolution. Although German policy under his direction was once again steady (in contrast, as he saw it, to the policies of U.S. presidents), the recession of 1981–82, with other frictions and difficulties, eroded his popular support and the coalition between his party and the Free Democrats.

So, on October 1, 1982, a temporarily exhausted Helmut Schmidt handed over the chancellorship to Helmut Kohl of the Christian Democratic Party and ceased to be the active political leader of the Social Democratic Party. In 1983 he announced that he would end his thirty-year career in the Bundestag at the next elections, presumably in 1987.

But it was quickly apparent that the voice that had dominated German politics and policy for a crucial eight years would not be stilled. Within his country he has remained the most respected political figure, and in Europe and the West generally—in the words of his friend Giscard d'Estaing—"the most esteemed German."

Only rarely is the label "great" accorded to a leader till his time at the top has receded—especially if that leader has been outspoken, quite often out of step with his party, and always ready to make tough decisions. Americans were slow to recognize the greatness of Harry Truman, as of Henry L. Stimson and Dean Acheson—all three fundamentally much like Schmidt.

Moreover, such men, having inevitably felt the storms of politics, are seldom forgivers and forgetters. In private Helmut Schmidt can be as blunt and caustic as his German political reputation—Trumanesque if you will—in reviewing the past, the actions of others, and on occasion his own. But if one measure of greatness is whether a statesman's real focus remains on the present and future, this test he meets to the full.

Schmidt set up his base in his native Hamburg, where he became the part-time co-publisher of the foremost German journal of opinion, the weekly *Die Zeit*. Leisure is not a word in his vocabulary; with intervals of extensive travel abroad (including China, the Middle East, and other key areas of the Third World), he has written trenchant leading articles for *Die Zeit, The Economist,* and other influential publications, while his rare speeches in the Bundestag have been carefully crafted and delivered to a packed chamber. A very large number of people who care, from all over the world, have beaten a path to his small house in the outskirts of Hamburg; none, I am confident, would disagree that the visit met Michelin's classic three-star criterion, "worth the trip." One emerges invigorated, stimulated by fresh ideas, sometimes exhausted—but always much the better.

But he has not, until this book, pulled his present thoughts together in systematic fashion. The invitation to do so by delivering one of Yale University's most prestigious lecture series, the Henry L. Stimson Lectures, was extended to him in the fall of 1983 by the Center for International and Area Studies at Yale. I had the honor (as a sometime Yale trustee and friend of the Center) of putting the possibility to the Chancellor in Hamburg on behalf of the director, William Foltz. After some consideration he agreed to deliver the lectures in the spring of 1985.

That the four lectures were, in Broadway terms, a box office sensation, was only one highlight of a visit that will live long in the memories of students and faculty alike. Schmidt spoke from notes, in pithy and almost flawless English that gained added force from the occasional German word ordering, to audiences that overflowed the largest halls in the University. After the lectures, he responded at length to questions, and in the evenings wore out smaller groups of faculty on special subjects such as arms control, the economic condition of Europe, and the interrelated issues that go to make up what he has called in this book the Grand Strategy of the West. As a sustained demonstration of energy, passionate concern, ordered thought, and articulate presentation, it was a performance not likely to be surpassed in any setting. It is a pleasure to record in print the immense appreciation of the University.

To outline at any length the arguments in this book would be presumptuous and could hardly do justice to them. Critical, often harshly critical, in his analysis of the present situation, Schmidt never shirks the obligation to propose alternatives. Thus, having argued throughout that purely national approaches and strategies are simply outdated and out of touch with the times and the nature of the world, he sums up, in the final chapter, a nineteen-point framework for a new Grand Strategy for the West. As an experienced politician, by instinct a pragmatist, Schmidt has no use for rhetorical castles in the air. Although at least two of his proposals call for sweeping change, for the most part he argues that the West has the institutions it needs, if it would only use them effectively.

In sum, this is an author of extraordinary experience and insight, addressing the central problems of today in a wholly constructive spirit. If individuals and particular policies are on occasion skewered, it is solely to make the argument that we, the nations of the West, can do a great deal better than we are now doing, and to point the way.

A GRAND STRATEGY FOR THE WEST

Henry L. Stimson Lectures
Yale University

1

The Absence of a Common Grand Strategy

I intend in this book to present a central thesis derived from my decade and a half of working experience in international affairs, namely, that national strategies are anachronistic in our present-day world. Or to put it more accurately: given the economic, political, and security interdependence of the Western world, neither the medium-size powers like Japan, France, Britain, Germany, Italy, and Canada, nor even the super-sized United States itself, can by their own national means alone achieve their economic goals, their political goals, or their external security.

For the most part they cannot even achieve their economic goals by joint action unless they also harmonize their political and security policies. Nor can they achieve external security simply by cooperating in defense or arms control; rather they must simultaneously harmonize their political and economic policies.

"Political internationalism without economic internationalism is a house built upon sand, for no nation can reach its full development alone." So wrote Wendell Willkie some forty-five years ago. Today, he might have added, not only is the converse true—that joint economic well-being requires also a high degree of political cooperation and mutual support—but both also require coordinated security policies.

To smaller countries the point has long been obvious. The less the international weight of a country, the greater its need to work with others. This can be clearly seen in the case of the three Benelux countries—Holland, Belgium, and the Grand Duchy of Luxembourg. Each would obviously fail if it tried to go it alone. Everyone in Brussels, or the Hague, or Luxembourg understands this and would consider it outdated nonsense even to think of a purely national economic policy, a purely national foreign policy, or a purely national security policy.

The bigger a country, on the other hand, the more tempted it is from time to time to try to act alone. General Charles De Gaulle succumbed to that temptation in French defense policy. But almost everyone in France today, including the French communists, realizes that there is no way France can defend itself without help. Because of Britain's experiences in this century, the British people too know that they cannot defend themselves alone. However, the majority of the British people still believe it is possible and worthwhile to try, again and again, to go their own way in *economic* policy. So far, this has resulted in three and a half million unemployed in Britain, more than were unemployed at the beginning of the depression over fifty years ago.

It is the United States, of course, that is subject to the greatest temptations. The impulse to act alone has historical and psychological roots in American isolationism. And from time to time it is nourished by disappointment in America's allies, or at other periods by an unbridled sense of the incomparable power of the United States—*The Arrogance of Power* was the book title chosen by Senator J. William Fulbright at such a period twenty years ago.

In any form it is a delusion to suppose that individual Western nations can be successful on a purely national basis. And it is equally a delusion to imagine that, even if they seek to act in cooperation, they can do so without having an agreed or accepted Grand Strategy.

What Does "Grand Strategy" Mean?

What do I mean by the word "strategy"? Nowadays, almost everyone claims to have a strategy. For the advertising managers of the soft drink industry it is a marketing or sales strategy, for football coaches a game strategy, or in America a "game plan." Professors of economics preach economic strategies to their governments, the World Bank offers a full set of development strategies, and of course the military in every country have military strategies, as they have had for three thousand years since the word strategy was first coined.

In order to avoid confusing these different meanings, I will speak separately of foreign policy, of economic policy, and of military strategy in the classic sense. Yet I do believe that all three must operate in the end within one and the same framework, whether we call that framework simply international relations or, in fancier language, the transnational fabric of the world of today. The goals that any nation, or group of nations, sets for itself *must* be consistent over all the three fields. They must, in short, be guided by a unifying concept, and this is what is meant by a Grand Strategy.

If I am not mistaken, the term "Grand Strategy" was introduced some three decades ago by B. H. Liddell Hart. This important British writer and thinker was originally an analyst of military strategy; he then developed and expanded his thoughts into the field of general political concepts, finding the two often closely, if not inextricably, related in the behavior of particular nations. One example of his insights, which Americans may feel hits pretty close to home, was the observation in his book *Strategy* that:

> Peaceful nations are apt to court unnecessary danger, because when once aroused they are more inclined to proceed to extremes than predatory nations. For the latter, making war as a means of gain, are usually more ready to call it off when they find an opponent too strong to be easily overcome. It is the reluctant fighter, impelled by emotion and not by calculation, who tends to press a fight to the bitter end.

That sounds very accurate to me. While Hart was writing about national behavior in wars, his comment helps, I think, to explain see-saw tendencies in U.S. policy that have been evident also in peacetime, especially in the kind of prolonged "twilight struggle"—as John F. Kennedy called it—in which the West and the Soviet Union have been engaged for nearly four decades. Americans do tend to want to get things over once and for all, to seek neat and lasting solutions especially through technology. At this very moment, is this not part of the reason for the way the Strategic Defense Initiative (or Star Wars) has been presented? I shall return to this and other issues of the present. Let me start, however, with a look at recent history, the record of the Western nations since World War II. It shows, I believe, four fairly distinct periods in which the West pursued broadly different types of Grand Strategy, with varying degrees of unity.

Four Phases of Western Grand Strategy

The first phase of Western Grand Strategy, which I call an *attempt at cooperation,* was rather short. This was the period right after the Second World War when the United States tried to achieve general cooperation with the Soviet Union. The United Nations was founded in San Francisco. An international monetary system was devised at Bretton Woods. The Baruch Plan offered the Soviets a share in the results of American research and development in the nuclear field (on lines earlier urged by Henry L. Stimson as he stepped down as Secretary of War). The Marshall Plan offered economic help to European and other countries, including the Soviet Union as well as former foes like my own country.

It was a phase in which America very quickly de-mobilized its military forces. But Stalin did not. Nor did he accept the Baruch Plan or agree to participate in the Marshall Plan. Rather, he laid the foundations for the nuclear weapons, shortly for the hydrogen weapons, and eventually for the rocketry and satellites of the Soviet Union. He forbade his client states in Eastern Europe to participate in the Marshall Plan. He tried to interfere in Greece, and to strangle Berlin, by blockading it for a year. All of these events led the West, under the leadership of Harry Truman, to found the Atlantic alliance in 1948 and 1949.

So this first phase was a short one in which the leading nation of the West offered cooperation to everyone, but the offer was not accepted by the Soviet Union. It quickly led instead to a second phase, which can be characterized by the catch words *"cold war"* and *"arms race."* It was also characterized by what came to be, under John Foster Dulles, a world-wide system of alliances around the Soviet Union. In the military field, the Western strategy was massive nuclear retaliation.

At the same time, several attempts were made to strengthen the West itself. In the early 1950s, there was a movement to found a European Defense Union; it failed. In 1957, the long effort to establish a European Economic Community brought about the Treaty of Rome; as we look back over the last thirty years, taken as a whole, that effort met with at least some success. It was always encouraged by the United States, which was at this stage totally dominant both militarily and economically and pursuing economic policies that were generally admired and accepted.

Yet the military component of the West's Grand Strategy in this cold war phase was never free of controversy and was indeed, by the late 1950s, the subject of profound dispute. I remember the enormous impact at that time of a book called *The Uncertain Trumpet*, by an outstanding American military man, Maxwell D. Taylor, who had just retired as U.S. Army chief of staff. Taylor raised crucial questions: we have the big nuclear trumpet, but what is going to happen if we don't blow the trumpet in time? Or if we feel inhibited from using it? Will the other side then win the conflict? And he concluded that the answers to these questions were uncertain, that one could not have confidence in the concept of massive retaliation, and that another military strategy and a different military posture were necessary.

Some thoughtful people in the West, less outspoken than General Taylor, had reached the same conclusion earlier. Others reached it later.

Be that as it may, Western leaders did come in the 1950s to the clear conclusion that Europe could not be defended without the assistance of a substantial German army. This led to the rearmament of West Germany. The rearming of the smaller, eastern part of divided Germany followed. In the Federal Republic, we now have about 500,000 soldiers under arms and could field 1.3 million soldiers within four or five days after mobilization.

Why did people think they needed soldiers to balance off the overwhelming masses of Russian conventional soldiers and tanks and artillery pieces? Because, in the meantime, it had become evident that the Soviet Union would reach equilibrium in mutual nuclear threats. The Berlin crisis, which reached its peak in 1961, and the Cuban missile crisis of 1962 illustrated this reality. Neither Washington nor Moscow (nor any of the allied or client states on either side) was willing to risk nuclear war—over Berlin or over Cuba—and they were right.

The realization that the Soviet Union and the West had reached equilibrium in their capacity to threaten each other with nuclear weapons led to a number of further insights, reaching far beyond the military field. A period of reassessment lasting almost a decade, from the late 1950s to 1967, ushered in the third phase of Grand Strategy, which some might call the phase of détente but which I will call the phase of *cooperation on the basis of assured security.*

In 1962, in the middle of the period of reassessment, President John F. Kennedy delivered a speech in Philadelphia still vividly remembered in Europe because he talked about the two pillars—the American pillar and the European pillar—on which the common Atlantic structure should rest in the future.

The growing understanding that a nuclear equilibrium, or balance of power, had been reached led to the first arms control negotiations between West and East and the first Test Ban Treaty in 1963, ending atmospheric tests. Five years later the Nuclear Non-Proliferation Treaty, negotiated by the Russians, the Americans, and the British, was signed; it was later adhered to by a great number of states throughout the world, which solemnly undertook not to acquire, produce, borrow, or buy nuclear weapons. The greatest breakthrough of all, of this kind, came in 1972 with the conclusion by Richard Nixon and Leonid Brezhnev of the first Strategic Arms Limitation Agreements, SALT I, which set agreed ceilings on intercontinental strategic missiles and, in particular, included the Anti-Ballistic Missile Treaty virtually banning entire ABM systems on both sides.

The official beginning of the third phase in the Grand Strategy of the West came at the end of 1967. The allied governments had set up a committee of foreign secretaries or their aides to try to define the grand strategic goals of the alliance. Under the chairmanship of the then Belgian foreign secretary, Pierre Harmel, the committee came up with a two-track philosophy that was then formally adopted by the North Atlantic Council. On one track, the Harmel Report clearly defined and declared the will of the Western allies to achieve their security by joint defensive effort and, through their defensive capability, to deter the Soviet Union from aggression. The second track, on the basis of that assured security, was to offer the Soviet Union cooperation, in the first instance in the area of arms control, by mutually

agreed-upon treaties, but also in the area of economic exchanges.

This double-track philosophy led also to the four-power agreement on Berlin between the United States, Britain, France, and the Soviet Union. It enabled my country, under Willy Brandt's chancellorship, to conclude treaties of non-use of force with the Soviet Union, with the People's Republic of Poland, with Czechoslovakia, and also with East Germany. These agreements went ahead to completion even though the Vietnam War was still being fought and Europeans were being rather critical of the role of the United States in Southeast Asia.

All this was possible also in spite of the fact that the world was starting to suffer from inflation, in the United States in the first instance because of the financing of the Vietnam War. The common thrust of Western strategy survived the collapse, in the early 1970s, of the Bretton Woods international monetary system, and of fixed exchange rates between the dollar and other important currencies, and continued even after the first oil shock of 1973–74 and the beginning of mass unemployment in the industrialized societies of North America and Western Europe. Indeed there was one great step forward in 1973, when Britain, not necessarily wholeheartedly, at last became a member of the European Economic Community.

The peak of this phase was reached in 1975, with the Helsinki Conference, in which almost all the European states participated, including the Soviet

Union, as a European power, and Canada and the United States, their claims to being European powers not having been disputed by the Soviet Union. This was the peak of that phase of cooperation in Europe, often called détente. The word, itself, by the way, had become official NATO language by the double-track philosophy adopted in 1967. Nowadays some people in America think it is a dirty word, but they are mistaken. They do not know enough of recent history.

By the time of the Helsinki Conference, the first oil shock of 1973–74 had led to a massive upheaval in the balance-of-payments system among the more than 140 nations of the world, including almost all the industrialized nations of the West. It was clear that an additional degree of economic cooperation was needed, and so it was, in fact, at Helsinki that it was resolved to introduce the so-called economic summits among the principal Western nations. I remember this very vividly because I was one of the two, along with President Giscard d'Estaing of France, who invented this whole endeavor. At Helsinki we had no great difficulty in convincing our American allies, President Gerald Ford and his Secretary of State, Henry Kissinger, and in short order had equally little difficulty in persuading the Japanese to participate. So the attempt to harmonize economic policies took on a new dimension at a time that was very dangerous in the economic sphere, and at the end of 1975 the first of the economic summits was held at Rambouillet on Giscard's invitation.

This third phase of Grand Strategy—military equilibrium and cooperation—began to unravel sometime after 1976. There were a number of reasons why it withered away: Soviet expansion in the Arab world and Africa, the Soviet-assisted invasion of Cambodia by the Vietnamese communists, and most dramatically the Soviet invasion of Afghanistan. Then, in the wake of Afghanistan, came the boycott of the Olympic Games in Moscow by the United States but not by any Europeans except for West Germany, Norway, and Turkey. In the meantime, by early 1977, the Soviet Union had begun an enormous buildup of a new intermediate-range missile, called the SS-20 in the West, which caused deep concern, as did the buildup of the Russian fleet.

All in all, it became clear that the network of agreements reached with the Soviet Union in 1970–73 did not cover the whole range of possible expansionist activity open to the Russians and that they were exploiting this fact. The agreements did cover mutual intercontinental nuclear threats and, more or less, geographically speaking, Europe (Berlin in particular), but they did not cover Southeast Asia, the Middle East, Africa, or Central America, to mention a few areas.

These developments, and especially the Soviet SS-20 buildup, led to the Western military counterstrategy of first announcing and then, after four years of unsuccessful negotiation, deploying additional American medium-range ballistic and cruise missiles on European soil. This led, in turn, to great

Russian concerns, in part over these new missiles (although their numbers were much smaller than the number of SS-20s), and even more by the statements made since 1980—which we in Europe heard as well as the Russians—about the necessity for superiority in the West, by the enormous boost in American defense budgets, and then in 1983 by the talk about Star Wars.

So, since the late 1970s, we have been in a fourth phase of Grand Strategy, namely, back at *cold war* and *arms race*—in a way back to Square Two, where we had been in the late 1940s and in the 1950s. Moreover, by sheer coincidence the close cooperation between the two leading Western European nations, France and Germany, that had grown up in the 1970s withered away after 1981, largely because of the departure of Giscard d'Estaing. Simultaneously, the second oil price shock hit the economies of almost all the Western industrialized countries, with the exception of Japan and a few Asian states like Taiwan, South Korea, Hong Kong, and Singapore, where the impact was slight. Most of the Western world sank into deep economic trouble, and we saw unemployment figures rising to orders of magnitude comparable to those of the early 1930s in the Great World Depression, which had such devastating social and then political consequences, like the coming to power of Hitler in Germany. If you have some 20 percent of the people unemployed, they tend to lose their political common sense.

Since 1977–78, several attempts have been made

to reach an arms agreement with the Soviet Union. One led to a draft treaty—SALT II—that was never ratified; because the Americans failed to ratify it, so did the Russians. Now the effort being made in Geneva may produce a positive result. I give it a 51 percent chance, which is quite high considering the experience of the last ten years. But no one can be sure. Today we are still in a cold war and arms race phase and in considerable economic difficulty in Europe.

To summarize the four phases: First, the phase of attempted cooperation. Second, the long phase of cold war and arms race. Third, the phase of assured security through military equilibrium accompanied by negotiation and cooperation with the Russians. Fourth, the new cold war and new arms race.

From a European point of view, one could say that the greatest degree of joint Grand Strategy in the West was achieved from the Truman administration to the end of the Kennedy administration. A fairly high level of joint strategy prevailed also during the Nixon-Ford-Kissinger era, though it characterized the West's relations with the Soviet Union more than the internal affairs of the Western nations. The degree of agreement on a basic approach to the Soviet Union was high after the Harmel Report and especially in the period from 1970 to about 1975, the time of the Helsinki meeting. After that détente came progressively to seem to many Americans to have been a delusion, or self-betrayal, a phase the Soviets had exploited to their own advantage, whereas Eu-

ropeans continued to see the double-track philosophy as basically sound and realistic.

So on both the political and economic fronts there
has been a progressive decay in common Western
Grand Strategy since 1977. The West's summit
meetings have deteriorated into television events.
Allies have been expected to perform ridiculous feats;
for example, the Japanese and Germans were expected to pull the vast economy of the United States
out of its inflationary and unemployment mess in
the late 1970s. Embargoes were decreed by one country, the United States, first on grain (lifted twelve
months later) and then on equipment for the natural
gas pipeline to the Soviet Union (lifted three months
later). All of this was done without shared infor-
mation—to say nothing of consultation—among the
allied governments.

Today, we in Europe are quite concerned about the
international economic consequences of the American budget deficits. First, Europeans are deeply worried about the high rates of interest—of *real* interest,
that is, interest over and above the inflation rate—
which are the highest the United States has seen
since the Civil War as well as the highest Europe
has seen in recent economic history. Second, they
are worried about the American trade deficit, which
leads to ever more pressure by those who want to
subsidize American exports or to restrict imports
into the United States and thereby diminish free trade
even further. Less then half the world's trade is free;
more than half is affected strongly by either subsidies

or protective measures. Third, Europeans are concerned about the enormous outflow of European savings and capital and credit to the United States. The richest country of the world has become the greatest net importer of foreign savings and of foreign capital, essentially in order to finance its budget deficits directly or indirectly.

None of this is really being dealt with among the allied governments. There is no joint strategy for coping with the economic mess in the world. Americans believe the world is in a period of economic upswing, but this is not true: the United States has seen an enormous economic upswing, true, but the rest of the world has not. Latin America has experienced the opposite, and the European economies— all of them—are stagnating, which is to a great degree due to the high real interest rates, which are not of their making.

Even in the military field the allied governments are not on the same wavelength. European governments have great misgivings about the Star Wars program. They do not voice this loudly, because they do not wish to appear to be having a dispute with their most important ally, but everyone in Paris or London or Bonn and everyone in Washington knows very well that there is no basic agreement in the alliance on the American Strategic Defense Initiative. Everyone in Europe and everyone in the Far East knows too that even if Star Wars hardware becomes a reality, it will not provide additional shelter or security to the nations of the Far East or of Europe.

It would be impossible for this kind of defense design to do so. This holds true also, of course, for the ASEAN countries (the Philippines, Indonesia, Thailand, Malaysia, and Singapore), which indirectly depend heavily on the capability of the United States and of the West as a whole to balance the military forces of the Soviet Union.

So the West today is far from united and far from pursuing truly joint policies either in the political and security areas or in the handling of economic problems. I have pointed out difficulties that arise from American policy, but a major feature of the present situation is also a set of attitudes in Europe, so that it is not carrying the responsibilities it should be carrying. This needs to be discussed at length, as it is especially hard for Americans to understand. But before we turn to that, let me detour briefly to say a special word about the situation of my own country.

The Special Situation of West Germany

It is difficult for most Americans to visualize the situation of West Germany. First of all, it is difficult to understand the enormous psychological wounds that the division of the German nation has caused—and the wounds are not healing. But let us leave that aside for the moment and focus simply on the military situation.

West Germany is a small country, about the size

of an average American state, say, Oregon or Colorado. But in Oregon or Colorado there are two or three million people. In West Germany there are sixty million. On top of that dense population there are, of course, military forces. I have mentioned our own forces numbering 500,000 soldiers; I should mention also the American forces, about 200,000, and French forces, British forces, Dutch and Belgian forces, Canadian forces, and even a Danish general. All of these are under a foreign high command.

Think of Oregon or of Colorado with six non-American forces, under a foreign high command, on their soil, and think also of the foreign high commander having some 5,000 nuclear weapons within his command and not under the host nation's control. Perhaps, if you reflect on that situation, you will understand why some young people in Germany, as well as older people and professors and bishops, protest our joint military posture. I am not a member of the peace movement, and I do not have the greatest sympathy for it, but I do have some understanding of why these people have grave misgivings. There is no other country in the world that has such a concentration of military weapons and military power from seven nations on its soil—and all of it under someone else's command.

I live in Hamburg, which is a port city at the estuary of the Elbe River where it flows into the North Sea. If I get in my car and drive eastward, it takes me about forty-five minutes to get to what is called the "Iron Curtain." If the Russians would let me pass, it would take me another thirty minutes to get to the barracks of the first Russian tank division. And, vice versa, it would take them only a little more than an hour to get to my home.

Think of the people in Oregon having seven different armies and 5,000 foreign nuclear weapons deployed on their soil, and the Russians that close! It takes the Soviet fighter bombers just five minutes to appear in the sky above Hamburg.

I hope this helps explain the situation of my country and why people living on the potential battlefield are not as cool about military threats and boasts as people living far from the Soviets on American soil may be. In the United States there are only American soldiers—no French, no British, no German, no Dutch, no Belgian troops. If there were, Americans might understand a little better the "Green" movement in West Germany, which has sprung up since the beginning of the second cold war and since the arrival of massive, long-lasting unemployment.

The Abdication of Europe

Returning to the subject of Europe as a whole, the plain fact I want to convey is that, for the time being, since their economic difficulties have become ever more pressing, the European governments have more or less ceased to play any role in framing a common approach to world politics or in articulating a Grand Strategy for the West. Whether the issue concerns the negotiations with the Soviet Union on intermediate-range nuclear missiles, including the famous "walk in the woods" of July 1982, whether it is Star Wars, or whether it is other aspects, such as strategic trade or the East-West cold war, the Europeans have more or less abdicated.

At this moment, I do not think this will last long, but it is a fact now. Yet at the same time the Europeans are rather concerned about what may be in the offing in the United States, what may be in the wings in the Pentagon or on the Hill in Washington or in the White House. As one American has phrased it, "It's not the possible crook that Europeans fear, but rather the honest man who they believe may not always know what he is doing."

There is a similar feeling in Japan, though to a lesser degree. Japan, of course, has fared much better economically than either the United States or Europe in the last fifteen years, mostly because the Japanese spend only 1 percent of their gross national product on defense, whereas we in Europe spend between 4 and 5 percent of our GNP every year, and the United States even more. Their relatively small defense budget leaves the Japanese enormous economic room to invest in capital improvements and productivity, and they do this very ably. They have found a niche in which to nest and hatch their economy. On the other hand, for their strategic defense they remain wholly dependent on the United States. Under the constitution installed after the war under

General MacArthur, they cannot build up a sufficient defense force of their own. Indeed, any effort
to do so would meet with the strong opposition of
the entire region. Both Koreas, China, the Philippines, Indonesia—all would oppose it. Japan does not
have close friends or allies in its region. It has only
one ally, and that one—the United States—is far
away. South Korea is in a similar situation, with no
close friends in the region. And even China—that
big nation with one billion people—has no friends
in the area.

China can afford not to have friends. For Korea, it
is a little more difficult. Koreans depend on America.
So do the Japanese. And so, to a high degree, do the
ASEAN nations. These are facts of life today, which
do not disturb Europeans. However, I do have to add,
parenthetically, that there is some uneasiness in Europe about the recent American discovery of the so-
called Pacific Basin, which is allegedly becoming the
most important focus of American geostrategic
thinking and even geostrategic engagement.

As for policy toward China—to which I shall return in more detail in the third chapter—European
governments have had a consistent China policy at
least since the late 1960s, when the word "China"
still meant Taiwan in the United States. The Europeans therefore felt comfortable with Nixon's
opening up of American relations with the People's
Republic of China in the early 1970s. But since then
we have been somewhat puzzled about aspects of

America's Far East policies; I personally have particular doubts about the perennial American pressure on Japan to change its economic behavior.

T *The Steady Grand Strategy of Soviet Russia*

he keystone of any coherent Western Grand Strategy must of course be the approach to the Soviet Union. And here the key point I want to stress is the deep historical roots, and resulting steadiness, of the Grand Strategy of Soviet Russia itself. It is worthwhile to look at historical maps to see how small the Grand Principality of Moscow was some five hundred years ago at the time of Ivan III or Ivan IV ("the Terrible"). Then look at the next map, say, at the end of the Thirty Years' War in Europe. Moscow had become quite a bit bigger by then. In the next map, at the time of the Vienna Congress of 1814–1815, Russia was reaching out to the south, having already moved out beyond the Urals and swallowed up the rest of Poland. And look at the map of today. Russia has grown and grown and grown—in the west from an ancient German city called Königsberg for centuries, now called Kaliningrad, to Kamchatka in the east, and even for a time including Alaska and going down the Pacific coast of what is now the United States to the Russian River, a couple of miles north of San Francisco. A very prudent American bought Alaska from Russia for $7.2 million; it was one of the rare occasions when the Russians withdrew from a territory they had taken.

For over five hundred years, all the Tsars pursued a policy known as "Gathering of the Russian Lands," which, practically speaking, meant conquering other people's land and afterward russifying the inhabitants. This Grand Strategy of cautious but continuous expansion has been continued and carried forward by the Soviet leadership of Russia. Contrary to much nonsense one can read in ideological papers and books about the Soviet Union, the Grand Strategy of Moscow is 75 percent traditional Russian strategy and only 25 percent communist strategy. For a man like Andrei Gromyko, who was foreign secretary for twenty-eight years until his recent elevation to the probably lesser role of President, spreading communist ideology has always been a means of carrying out Russian Grand Strategy. Mikhail Suslov, the keeper of ideological purity, would have thought a bit differently, of course, but there are differences of opinion about strategy in every country. In the Soviet Union the traditional and historical thrust has always, in my view, been the dominant one.

If it is true that this thrust for expansion has persisted for five centuries, it is obviously necessary to contain the further expansion of the Soviet Union. The word "containment," readers may recall, was coined shortly after World War II by an outstanding American strategic thinker, George Kennan, who was a diplomat at that time. I have no doubt that containing Russian expansion should still be a very important component of Western Grand Strategy.

On the other hand, living close to the Iron Curtain, having lived close to the Russians for over a thousand years, we in Europe are rather careful not to give them the impression that we are preparing to overwhelm them. We never could, and we do not wish either to scare them or to get into a war of mutual scaring. Nor do we wish to get into a war of economic attrition. My city of Hamburg has lived on sea trade for over a thousand years, and for many centuries Novgorod was one of our trading partners. So were other cities around the Baltic Sea and the North Sea; only in the last four hundred years has the main emphasis of our foreign trade shifted toward Africa, Asia, and America.

In the cultural sphere we have always been close to each other, and so have Americans, though they do not really recognize it. I cannot conceive of concert life in Boston or New York or Chicago or Los Angeles without Tchaikovsky, Moussorgsky, Rimski-Korsakov, Shostakovich, and Prokofiev. I cannot imagine any of us, anywhere in the world, living in the world of culture or studying the culture of the nineteenth century without feeling at home with people like Dostoevski, Tolstoi, Lermontov, Pushkin, Turgenev, Gogol, and nowadays Pasternak and Solzhenitsyn. The Russians have contributed a lot to our Western civilization, as we in Italy, France, Germany, England, and America have contributed to theirs.

This mutual nourishment, or fructification, leads a European to want to maintain neighborly relations and not, again and again, to increase enmity and suspicion and fear. This is why most Europeans and European governments —whether conservative, liberal, socialist, or social democratic—want to return to the double-track philosophy vis-à-vis the Russians that I dealt with earlier, that is, to make whatever effort is necessary to feel secure against Russian pressure or blackmail or attack, and, with that security as a foundation, to cooperate with them. Moreover, it is this double-track philosophy that the Hungarians, the Poles, the East Germans, the Czechs, and the Rumanians are most interested in. Such a Western strategy would give them more room for autonomous decisionmaking and for autonomous development. And vice versa: the greater the polarization within Europe between West and East, the smaller the already limited range of freedom the nations in Eastern Europe, now suffering from the division of the continent, will enjoy.

At this time, Europeans are profoundly skeptical of the amount of careful thinking that lies behind the Grand Strategy of their most important ally and friend. They see, and worry about, a pattern of volatility and discontinuity in American strategy in recent years. On the other hand, for the time being the Europeans have abandoned their own natural interest in full participation in the shaping of the West's common Grand Strategy. So I shall return, in my last chapter, to what may be the ultimate questions: Can the United States alone define and implement Western Grand Strategy, and if so to what extent? Or is such an undertaking in itself inherently anachronistic and futile?

2

Europe's Role and Problems

As I have just stated, Europe has, in the last couple of years, abdicated its role as a participant in the formulation of the West's Grand Strategy. This abdication—at a time of heightening tension, when a second cold war characterizes relations between Moscow and Washington—reflects all too clearly a present weakness of Europe. Europe still has enormous economic, financial, monetary, industrial, and military potential. But its potential is unrealized, because leadership is lacking, whether we have in mind cooperation among the Western European states and joint Western European leadership or leadership by a single country or even by a single leader's personality. All of this could happen in Europe, but it is not there today.

To those who are impatient with Europeans, I would like to point out that the United States is only a little over two hundred years old and has had the same language for over two hundred years, while most of the European states are much, much older. Italy goes back more than two thousand years, France more than a thousand years, Poland exactly a thousand years, Germany a little more than a thousand years, Britain a thousand years. And the languages in all of these countries have been different from each other for periods longer than a millenium. The process of differentiation of cultures has been going on for unthinkably long periods. It is simply not possible to overcome the heritage of centuries by a snap of the fingers or even by the moving speech of one real statesman.

It is likely, therefore, that it will take many long years for the Europeans to arrive at anything like a European Union. I am a pragmatist and have never been given to Sunday speech making. I doubt that I will see a European Union in my lifetime, but close cooperation among Europeans could be achieved. It would enable them to stand up against those American ideas that are wrong for Europe.

Americans are wrong if they believe that what's good for America must always be good as well for Europe. And what's good for Europe is not necessarily good for America. And what's good for Japan is not necessarily good for America. And what's good for America is not necessarily good for Japan. What is needed is that one have first a clear picture of one's own national interests but second the will to compromise with the national interests of one's partners or allies or friends. This, of course, makes it necessary for all to speak their minds clearly—which is not the case today.

I do not see Western Europe as finally and irreversibly in decline. However, I have to admit that, as a result of its lack of internal cohesiveness and leadership, Europe is now increasingly losing economic and political, as well as military, weight in the world. Someone once said, "It is an immense advantage to have done nothing, but one should not abuse it."

Europeans have not done much in the last couple of years, but they should not abuse it.

What are the underlying reasons for Europe's decline in the last ten years, especially the last couple of years? Can these underlying factors be overcome, in the face not only of recurring old problems but also new and oncoming ones? What, in short, are the prospects for Europe and for its role in the world as we approach the end of the twentieth century and look even further into the future?

I will deal with this set of questions in three parts: first, the military and arms control sphere; second, the economic and financial issues; and third, the historical and political framework.

I

Security Dilemmas

In the first chapter I discussed the broad expansionist thrust of Soviet policy. I shall not try to present a detailed picture of the Soviet military threat and potential but will only remind the reader of a few central facts about the military threat to Western Europe.

First, there is the fact of Soviet superiority in numbers of soldiers, tanks, artillery pieces, close ground-support aircraft, rockets and aircraft for interdiction, and so on. In the area between the Soviet Union and the western coast of Europe there is not a satisfactory military equilibrium in terms of numbers of forces or quantities of equipment.

Second, there is an even greater disequilibrium if one takes into account not only the troops present on the central European battlefield but also the great mobilizable reserves of military manpower in the Soviet rear that can be brought forward within a fortnight. The West clearly has much smaller reserves of soldiers. There is no draft in the United States or in Britain, so these two states have no considerable reserves at all. It would take them two years to build up their reserves, as it did in the two world wars. France and Germany do have large reserve forces, but France has put all its troops, including its reserves, outside the NATO military framework. Therefore, taking into account the reserves on the Soviet side and on the Western side, there is a considerable imbalance in conventional military forces in Europe.

Third, new threats have arisen since the 1970s. I have in mind the SS-20 and SS-22 missiles. The intermediate-range SS-20s, in particular, now have about a thousand independently targetable nuclear warheads, and these are supplemented by several thousand nuclear weapons of shorter range, all pointed at West European targets. On the Western European side, there are a limited number of French and British nuclear weapons, which would not mean much against the vast numbers on the Soviet side, and, on the part of the United States, a few hundred warheads on intermediate-range nuclear ballistic and cruise missiles, plus some 5,000 shorter-range nuclear weapons (almost exclusively, by the way, on

German soil). In other words, in the area of nuclear weaponry, no equilibrium is possible in the European theater without the American nuclear component present there. This will not change in the future, because the European nations, except France and Britain but including Germany, have undertaken by signing and ratifying the Non-Proliferation Treaty not to produce or buy nuclear weapons or have them under their national control.

In this situation the first question is how to defend Western Europe in case of a prolonged conventional attack that involves all the mobilizable Soviet reserves. Until Robert McNamara's Athens guidelines of 1962, or more properly the formal revision of NATO doctrine in 1967, the strategic answer had been resort to "massive nuclear retaliation" in case of such a Soviet attack. McNamara realized by 1962 that this strategy was no longer feasible, and the rest of the alliance came to share this view by 1967 at the latest. And because the Western alliance itself did not consider it feasible, it was also not credible to the Russians. Since 1967, therefore, the declared strategy of the alliance has been "flexible response"—that is, to try to hold the Russians for at least a couple of days (I would rather hope for a couple of weeks) by conventional defense and then resort rather early to Western first use of so-called tactical nuclear weapons. (I refer to them as "so-called" because in fact they are lethal and deadly weapons for the German and Polish populations living on the battleground. Indeed, I personally resent a terminology that calls weapons that kill Americans "strategic" and weapons that kill only Poles or Germans "tactical." It is a belittling term for a category of weapons that, if used in great numbers, will kill or cripple the greater part of the Central European peoples.)

In the years since 1967, the "early first use" strategy has become more and more of a problem, raising in particular the question whether it is acceptable to those most concerned. To accept such a military strategy for Europe may be easy for someone who lives in California or Georgia. It is not so easy—it is almost impossible—to accept it if you are living in the center of Europe.

This matter of acceptability—or rather the principle that one's own strategy has to be acceptable to the nations one wants to defend—is in my view one of six main principles of military strategy that one has to bear in mind if one is evaluating the scene from the European point of view. These principles could and should be shared by Americans.

1. The first principle is the principle of *deterrence.* Deterrence is not a new invention of the twentieth century. As a strategic principle, it has played a role ever since the time of the ancient Greeks and Romans: deter the potential aggressor by threatening him with some evil that outweighs his possible gains.

2. The second principle is the principle of plausibility or *credibility.* The adversary has to be made to believe that you are really going to do what you are threatening to do. This is now the crux of all our

nuclear strategies. To the extent that doubts arise in the West about the feasibility of our military strategy, these are bound to create doubts on the Soviet side about the credibility of our threat to them.

3. The third principle I call the principle of appropriateness or *proportionality of the means* we intend to use in our defense strategy. One can say that the debate on the question, what is proportionate, or, how much is enough, has become more serious and more important and is today playing a more central political role than in any of the earlier phases of Western strategy since 1945.

4. The fourth principle is that of regular or constant *reevaluation*, because situations do change. We have to revise our evaluations constantly. As the history of the first thirty-five years of NATO has shown, we have from time to time revised our military strategy, and we will have to do so again in the future.

5. The fifth principle is the principle of *equilibrium*—or a rough balance of security for each side. It is this principle that brings into play the necessity of efforts to arrive at mutually agreed-upon arms limitations. Begun in the late 1960s, this endeavor met with considerable success in the first half of the 1970s but no further success since then; SALT II, worked out in 1979, was not ratified by the United States and therefore not by the Russians either. All the other arms control negotiations at all the different tables in Vienna and Geneva in the last twelve years have failed.

Some of the questions that arise in arms limitation negotiations are the following: What is proportionate? What will be proportionate tomorrow? How do we find an equilibrium? How do we stabilize equilibrium after we have defined or found it? What are the necessary ingredients of an agreement? Obviously no superpower, and no smaller power like Germany, would ever subscribe to an agreement that seemed on balance to offer advantages to the other side. And obviously the other side would never subscribe to an agreement that offered advantages to our side. So the principle of equilibrium is inherently present in any effort to get an arms limitation agreement between the two sides. It is easy to state this but very difficult for some political leaders to understand and accept.

6. Finally, there is a sixth principle, of *acceptability*, which is closely related to the second principle, of credibility. Doubts about our military posture and plans are indeed growing today. To put it another way, there is a growing deficit within our own public opinion. Whether in our parliaments—in the Senate of the United States, in the German Bundestag, in the British House of Commons—whether in our churches or within our universities, whether among those who consider themselves experts or in the public at large—in many, many places within our public opinion the evidence of this deficit is mounting steadily. It is what lies behind the several types of freeze proposals, including those for a unilateral freeze; behind proposals to adopt "no first

use" or "no early first use" strategies; behind the
struggle over additional MX missiles in the United
States and the earlier struggle over the deployment
of Pershing II ballistic missiles and ground-launched
cruise missiles (the latter still continuing in Holland); and, today, behind the controversy over President Reagan's Strategic Defense Initiative. In short,
our present military posture and strategy are not
really convincing to our own publics, our own politicians, or our own political elites.

It is crucial to realize that if we cannot convince
our own publics, if we cannot convince our own
parliaments, then we run the risk of very dangerous
misunderstandings and miscalculations on the Soviet side—miscalculations about what we really
might do in the event of blackmail or attack or violation of our borders. Our own controversies and
doubts might even, under certain circumstances,
seem to be an invitation to them to act.

So the issues of acceptability and proportionality
are today at the heart of the European security problem. Our strategies will be and remain credible only
if we accept them ourselves and only if there is no
sensible or substantial opinion in our own countries
that does not accept them. Now that public opinion
has been awakened to all these problems, I prophesy
that for the rest of the century, and even into the
next century, the West will never again be in a position to adopt a military strategy or military posture
that is not acceptable to our own public because it
seems inevitably to destroy what we wish to defend.

But if early first use of nuclear weapons is an increasingly unacceptable military strategy to the European nations living in the battleground, the question inevitably arises: How can they create a situation in which early first use of nuclear weapons becomes unnecessary? Or in which the choice of using nuclear weapons first is shifted to the Soviet side?

The answer in the first instance is that one needs equilibrium in conventional forces, either by adding Western forces (and not reducing Western forces, as Senator Mike Mansfield proposed some twenty years ago and Senator Sam Nunn proposes today) or by agreements between West and East on mutually balanced forces and then, hopefully, a reduction of forces to a lower level on each side. An effort has been made to achieve this, under the name of Mutual Balanced Force Reduction (MBFR), at the negotiating table in Vienna for over a dozen years without result. The prospect of getting an MBFR agreement does not seem great at this time.

It seems to be a general conviction of many in the United States that, in order to be able to defend oneself, one has to spend as much money for defense as one can. In my view, this is not the right perspective. If our main difficulty is Soviet superiority in ability to conduct conventional warfare, what we need is not to spend more money for nuclear or space warfare but to get appropriate numbers of soldiers and conventional weapons on our side. What matters most is the necessity to defend ourselves by conventional means.

And here the first priority is soldiers, not money. The second priority is motivation for our soldiers, again not money. The third priority is education, training, and skills for our soldiers, still not money. Only the fourth priority—boots, guns, vehicles, tanks, and what-have-you to equip the soldiers—requires money.

Men matter most, not only in the pragmatic sense of actual experience in warfare but also in a moral and philosophical sense. It is my conviction that, in defending itself against foreign violence, a democracy must not rely on volunteers or on mercenaries, but every citizen ought to understand that he himself has to sacrifice some part of his life to maintain a secure defense. I understand the feeling of many Americans that conscription was misused during the war in Vietnam. But just to abandon the draft forever is too easy a way out of a domestic controversy. None of the continental nations of Western Europe has taken that road. They have maintained conscription, which in political terms involves a much greater individual sacrifice than spending taxpayers' money.

It is largely because the continental European nations have stuck to this politically difficult course, while the United States has not, that I do not consider legitimate the many American criticisms of the defense expenditures of the European countries as too small. I see as even less legitimate American threats to reduce the number of American soldiers in Europe in order to force European governments to spend more.

Obviously the United States is not going to change its military thinking and its order of priorities in the short run. Therefore the Europeans themselves ought to look at their situation.

Here there is one central problem, in particular, that stands in the way of a truly effective European defense effort. If France would bring its conventional forces and reserves into the joint framework of Western defense, it would be easy to achieve a satisfactory equilibrium in conventional forces between Western Europe and the Soviet Union. After mobilization, we would then have some eighteen German divisions, some fifteen to eighteen French divisions, plus several Benelux divisions—altogether up to forty Western European divisions—plus perhaps one or two American divisions and some British forces as well. Such a force would, of course, have to be placed under a French supreme commander.

It is one of the monstrosities of the present situation in Europe that many hundreds of thousands of drafted European soldiers, who are under American supreme command, are being told, time and again, that they could not fight successfully for very long, so the West will be forced to use tactical nuclear weapons and thereby destroy their home countries.

If we desire to improve that awkward situation, another question arises, namely, how does one persuade the French political leadership, whose assessment of strategic matters is still made under the dominating spiritual shadow of Charles De Gaulle, to take the basic step I have just suggested? De Gaulle believed that France should act independently, hoping—but not saying this publicly—that others would be in the forefront defending Western Europe, including France. If the French were to decide on a new policy (perhaps by sheer necessity, for instance because the United States withdrew, which is a very big if), only then might there be a need for considerable budget money to buy additional weapons for all of its mobilizable reserves, additional vehicles, additional ammunition, and so on.

A *Economic Dilemmas*

Americans read in their newspapers about the European Common Market, and something like that really does exist among ten nations. Spain and Portugal will soon become full members of the European Economic Community as numbers eleven and twelve. But if you look closely enough, you will see that it is not really a common market. The French telephone and telegraph system will not buy German telephones, British Rail will never buy French rail cars, the German federal railroad system will not buy British locomotives, and so on. It is said to be a common market, but it is not really very common! There is neither a common tax system in that market of 275 million people, nor is there a common set of technical standards. There is not even a coordinated taxation policy in the ten countries. Except for the rather small budget of the Brussels secretariat and for agricultural policies, there is no joint budget framework for the member states, nor do the finance ministers of the member states have a coordinated budgetary policy.

There is no joint currency, nor is there even a coordinated set of monetary policies for the ten finance ministers and ten central banks. There is a beginning of commonality in the monetary field— the so-called European Monetary System created at the end of the 1970s under the joint leadership of France and Germany—but governments are rather reluctant these days to complete the system and make it a factor and a force in the international credit market and the international currency network.

What does exist is in the main a joint agricultural price system and farmers' income policy. A stupid one, by the way—no better than American agricultural policy. It eats up about 66 percent—perhaps even 70 percent—of all the budget money of the European authorities in Brussels. The fact that joint agricultural policy dominates the EEC stems from a mistake that was made very early, some thirty years ago, in the Treaty of Rome itself. The consequence is that every year the ministers of ten countries struggle more over income differentials for European farmers than over anything else.

But farmers number only 7½ percent of the population of Europe, whereas more than 11 percent of the people of Europe are unemployed at present, which creates much bigger problems than the income problems of farmers. There is no common solution in sight for the 11-plus percent unemployed. Instead, in the last few years, since the second oil price shock, several governments have made limited attempts to reduce unemployment in their countries on a purely national basis.

France, for example, has done this. When President Mitterrand came into office in the spring of 1981, France deliberately embarked on a strong change of policy toward deficit spending. Its leaders were thinking, along classical Keynesian lines, that this would create additional demand, that goods would have to be produced to meet the demand, and that this would then create jobs in productive industries. Well, it did so to some extent, but mainly it created or preserved jobs for Germans and Italians, because their industrial enterprises were more flexible in providing goods for the French market than the state-owned French industries. So what France got was an enormous deficit in its balance of trade and current account. The French government had to devalue the franc three times in less than two years; after that, it gave up on deficit spending policy altogether. Unemployment has not been reduced in France but has since increased.

The United Kingdom is another example. Prime Minister Thatcher has tried to carry out a true national supply-side economic policy for some years but clearly with even less positive results than the

French have had. Britain has even higher numbers and higher percentages of unemployed.

Holland is a third example. It has tried to follow Germany, because most of its exports go to Germany; Germany is its biggest and most important market. But in its attempt to follow German monetary policies, it has created for itself more than 16 percent unemployed. Italy, on the other hand, virtually prints money as it needs it and therefore has one of the highest inflation rates in Europe. Germany has always done a little better than the rest with inflation—it has never seen double-digit inflation rates—and with unemployment as well. But Germany's economic performance since 1981 has also been unsatisfactory.

Despite all these difficulties, these 275 million (in the future more than 300 million) people are potentially an enormous market. It is as large a population as that of the United States, even a little larger. And to give a feeling for the economic potential, let me mention that just one of these ten or twelve countries—Germany—exports about the same volume of goods as the United States, although the population of the United States is four times as large. Germany even exports a larger volume of goods than Japan, although Japan has twice the population. And France, the United Kingdom, Holland, Italy, and the others are exporting a large volume of goods as well.

I stress these points to illustrate that there is an enormous world market potential in that old European continent. But the futile attempt of the individual European countries to pursue national instead of common economic policies is highly anachronistic. Not one has met with success in the different national mixes of fiscal and monetary policy that have been tried since the second oil price shock of 1979–80.

Under these circumstances, what is necessary and what is possible in the near future? Three different steps are at least thinkable.

1. First, one could certainly create a true common market in order to enjoy the advantages of economies of scale. For example, literally by a stroke of the pen one could make procurement by all governments and their agencies and state-owned corporations a truly European affair, a truly open competition for anyone inside Europe. It could be done easily and would easily lead to greater cooperation among national, private, and state-owned enterprises alike.

2. Second, one could quickly strengthen the European Monetary System. This would not need a treaty that would have to be ratified; it could be done instead by agreement among the governments or even among the central banks alone. The purpose would be to bring about a greater convergence of the monetary policies of central banks as part of a broader convergence of the economic policy mixes of the individual governments, which would have to behave in order not to be forced into devaluations or upward valuations of their respective currencies. In other words, the goal would be to harmonize the economic behavior of participating governments in

the fiscal and monetary fields, and to create a really common market with respect to the money, or currency, being used.

If you travel from New Haven to New York, you use the same greenback. Or if you go from New York to Orlando and from there to Beverly Hills and then to Seattle, you still use the same greenback. This is not the case in Europe, where you have to change your money at every border. And some of the European states have very restrictive monetary policies, while others change their policies from time to time. We are way behind the true common markets that exist within the United States and inside Japan. The Japanese have one currency for a market of 120 million people, the Americans one currency for 235 million people. But we in Europe have ten currencies for 275 million people!

Strengthening the European Monetary System would also enable the European Economic Community, as an entity, to stand up to the presently overwhelming weight of the economic mix of policies in the United States—the *économie dominante*, as the French call it. That mix, combining restrictive monetary policy on the one hand with super-Keynesian deficit fiscal behavior on the other hand, has brought about what are, in real terms (that is, after inflation), the highest interest rates ever, if you look at the world as a whole. In the immediate future a strengthened European Monetary System could help Europe stand up to American policy. At the same time the goal of such a strengthening of the EMS, in the long run, would be to create a kind of triangle of the main currencies in the world—the American dollar, the European écu, and the Japanese yen.

3. A third, and even more difficult, step would be for the Europeans to agree on common economic behavior or action to restructure the European economy, so that it would again have enough quantitative and qualitative growth to foster competitiveness and restore a high level of employment. To a much greater degree than the American economy, the European economy is geared toward construction and producing goods for fixed capital investment. There is a much higher proportion of old smokestack industries in England, France, Belgium, Holland, and the Ruhr than there is in America, even in, say, Pittsburgh or Cleveland or Detroit.

Large parts of Europe's industry, which have been heavy up to now, badly need restructuring. We will not see again the enormous demand for steel that we saw during the Vietnam War. Nor the enormous demand for ships and vessels of all kinds that prevailed during the Vietnam War and the intense conflicts of 1967–73 between Israel and its neighbors; since the reopening of the Suez Canal, we have not needed tankers of 400,000 or 500,000 tons. So instead of an obsolete capacity in shipbuilding and steel, Europe needs modern industries with a potential for growth, whether it be in new technologies or in services. And certainly Europe needs a joint high-tech research and development program.

President Mitterrand has recently made a number

of proposals for large joint projects that should be undertaken, like a network of fast trains connecting the main cities of Europe—trains running at speeds like those of the trains between Tokyo and Osaka and between Paris and Lyon. The tunnel could at last be built under the channel between England and the Continent. Joint civilian space and telecommunications projects could be undertaken, and so forth. As the Europeans cannot, to the same large extent as the Americans, use their defense budgets to boost high technology all over their industrial society, they have to achieve similar results by means of joint civilian projects. Mitterrand also has launched a joint European high-technology effort under the name "Eureca." All these initiatives point in the right direction.

The question, of course, is whether any of the three initiatives I have suggested will be taken in the near future. The problem is that the awareness, or imagination, is lacking in most of the current European administrations. And where some of the awareness exists, the will is missing. And where there might be some of the will, the skill to implement it is absent. In general, Europe lacks political vitality today.

The Political Framework of Western Europe

Some readers may ask themselves at this point the simple question: Why can't the nations of Europe live as one big family? My answer is that they try to, they really try. But as nations in time of war hate their enemies, so do they in time of peace sometimes hate their friends and relatives. (No doubt this is true even in some American families.) European nations sometimes cannot understand American foreign policy; if at times Americans cannot understand the behavior of the European family of nations, well, that makes us even! I do admit, though, that it is not so easy to understand the inhibitions that hold Europe back today.

Speaking of friends who occasionally behave as enemies, or rather as nationalistic competitors, I should add that the Western European nations today—plus the Poles, the Hungarians, the Czechs, and others in Eastern Europe—do feel themselves to be friends even though they have behind them a millenium of rivalry and war. In this respect, the European situation is far preferable to the condition of the Far East or the Middle East, where all too many nations do not really want to be close friends. This is indeed one enormous difference between the complex situation in Europe and the equally complex situations in the Middle East, the Far East, and South Asia.

For example, a public opinion poll taken in France today on the question, "Who is our best friend?" will result in an almost two-thirds majority answering, "It is the Germans." If you take the same public opinion poll in Germany, more than 70 percent of the Germans will answer, "Our best friends are the

French." Both results were unthinkable thirty years
ago. That is enormous progress. In some ways the
people have made greater progress than their political leaders.

I must confess that I have been a rather francophile
German political leader, although I am not a fran-
cophone individual (I use the English language when
I talk to my French friends). I have not always been
a francophile. Almost thirty years ago, in 1957, when
the Treaty of Rome that set up the European Economic Community was before the German parliament for ratification, I abstained from voting because
I then thought—much as I was convinced of the necessity of European integration—that the EEC could
never be successful in the absence of British experience and pragmatism.

In the intervening thirty years I have had a lot of
disappointments as well as positive experiences. One
of the former has been to learn that almost no woman
or man in England's political class, whether belong-
ing to the right wing or the left wing of the political
spectrum, and almost no woman or man in office in
Whitehall, thinks that the Atlantic Ocean between
England and America is broader than the channel
between England and continental Europe. (The one
notable exception, of course, was Edward Heath, but
he has been out of office for more than twelve years;
there have been a few other exceptions among people
who are in the opposition.) On balance, I have come
to think that General De Gaulle was right in his
belief that the British are not really prepared to cast

their lot with the rest of the European nations. As far as the integration of Western Europe is concerned, the British have never taken the advice of George Bernard Shaw, who once said, "The people who get on in this world are the people who get up and look for the circumstances they want, and if they can't find them make them." The British will join the club only if they cannot prevent it from being successful. (If this sounds harsh, I apologize to the British.)

I started out in operational politics as an anglophile, but this kind of experience, as well as the impact of President John F. Kennedy, led me to become politically an Americanophile, or, as one was called in those years in Europe, an "Atlanticist." Then, not because of disappointment with our Atlantic American partners but more as a consequence of my own insight into the geopolitical situation of my country, during the last fifteen or eighteen years I have become in the end a francophile, a convinced advocate of the priority of friendship and close economic, political, and military cooperation between France and Germany.

I referred earlier to the military situation on German soil and touched on the battlefield character of my country. I must now add what many French and other West Europeans do not fully grasp, at least consciously, namely, that the Germans carry a heavy burden from the great injury, the severe wounds inflicted upon them with respect to their national identity. To divide a nation by force does not create two nations. It can destroy a nation; but in the German case it has wounded the nation deeply without destroying it. The East and West Germans share a profound wish to be reunited under one roof sometime in the future. No one should have any illusions—the Germans will be as stubborn as the Poles, who got together again after having been divided for almost 130 years. Shortly thereafter they were divided once more by Stalin and Hitler, but still they desired to get together and after 1945 prevailed even under very disadvantageous circumstances. The same will come true for the Germans, though they know there is no chance of it in the presently foreseeable future. It may come sometime in the next century, perhaps late in the next century.

At the same time, we Germans know that the Russians are and will remain our neighbors, powerful neighbors. As I have already pointed out, they are very close by—just five minutes away by fighter-bomber plane if they want to drop bombs on my city of Hamburg and just an hour away for their first tank division if they should decide to march westward. For many long centuries they have been our neighbors, and because they will continue to be so we Germans want to have normal relations and live in peace with them. It is easy to describe a faraway state as an "empire of evil," but if that state is your immediate neighbor you will be much more careful in choosing your words. To be frank, this is why we and other Europeans do not like such language.

We also know that we have to be on our guard against our Russian neighbors—able to defend ourselves and, by this capability, deter them from any conceivable violation of our borders. Germans know full well that they cannot do this alone, that they need partners and allies. There are about 60 million Germans on the western side of Germany (plus about 16 million on the eastern side), but the Soviets number 270 million.

In particular, German interests within Europe can be pursued only to the extent that the French are involved and support them. On the other hand, France wants to play a great role on the world stage. It is thought in Paris and in France that after centuries of continuous spiritual and political development it is natural and legitimate for France to play a world role. But a nation of 55 million people cannot play such a role effectively if it does not have friends and allies who follow French leadership. So I think it is in the interest of both France and Germany for the two countries to work as closely together as they can. Alone, each one is too small to carry important weight vis-à-vis the two giants, whether it is the unfriendly neighbor in the east or the friendly ally in the west or, in the future, the oncoming world power, China, which will have a population of more than 1.2 billion by the end of the century.

In speaking of France and Germany, one must not forget the history that lies between these two nations. Only after innumerable wars have they become willing to see each other today as best friends. That is a great thing. In this relationship the strength of the German position arises to some extent out of the paradox of its geopolitical situation. Germany has more neighbors than friends. It also has had more neighbors during the last couple of centuries than any other nation in the world except China. No other nation on earth is situated in the middle of such a small continent, with so many neighbors surrounding it. This is one of the reasons why there have been so many wars. Sometimes the Germans have lashed out beyond their borders, and sometimes peoples from the north (the Norsemen and Vikings), or from the west (the French under Louis XIV and Napoleon), or from the east (the Hungarians, the Turks, the Russians) have invaded Germany. Most devastatingly and criminally under Hitler the Germans tried to conquer their neighbors.

The geopolitical position of Germany, as well as the perception of it as the battleground in the military strategic thinking of both the Soviet Union and the West, makes it indispensable for the West that Germany be politically oriented toward the West and bound closely to it. If this bond should be broken, it would be a critical loss for the West, for which nothing else could make up. However, in the long run the Germans will remain on the Western side only if the French help them and bind them to the West. This heartland of continental Europe will not be bound to the West by an American president coming from Georgia, California, or any other state; it can be tied to the West only by the West Europeans, by the French in particular.

French leaders, whether De Gaulle or Pompidou

or Giscard d'Estaing or Mitterrand, have understood this and have accepted it as a necessity in their political behavior. But the French do not yet understand that they cannot continue to ask the Germans to bear the risks of defending France against the East unless France too participates fully and visibly in that endeavor. France can lead Germany only if it shares in the risks and in the actual defense. It can lead politically only if it also participates in the military leadership, which of course presupposes participation in the joint military effort as a whole.

As long as France does not wish to make that move, which is difficult to make in the still-Gaullist mood in France's strategic thinking today, the Germans will continue to think of the French as their best friends, but they will not think of France as their most important military ally. Rather they will continue to consider the United States as occupying that role.

It is deeply in the general interest of the West, as well as of the Germans (including the East Germans), for this central European heartland to be tightly bound to the Western family, or the Western alliance. This is especially important in order to avoid a situation in which a single European state falls victim to Russian hegemony or in which, because of the neutralization of Germany or parts of Germany, Soviet Russia's advantage in numbers of conventional forces gains additional political weight. Today it seems beyond question that a genuine and lasting coupling of West Germany and the West has really occurred. There is no doubt about this in Germany and no good reason for foreigners to doubt it. On the other hand, Western Europe has not become an effective economic unit, largely because of British reluctance. Nor has Western Europe become an effective defense unit, because of French reluctance.

C *American Dominance*

ertainly Europe has not increased its autonomy vis-à-vis the United States. Indeed, the contrary seems to be true in the last couple of years, especially since the United States has overcome its psychological weakness after Vietnam and Watergate.

As we approach the end of the century, the American-Soviet bipolar world may be gradually changing into a triangular world power constellation; I will address this subject later. But I wish to stress here that Europe does not seem at this time to have the will to play a role in that world league in which we find the United States, the Soviet Union, and, in the future, the People's Republic of China. Most West Europeans still delude themselves by looking at the world from a Eurocentric perspective. History has been written from a Eurocentric perspective for two thousand years, and Europeans have not given up the habit. They find it difficult to understand that history is happening on other continents as well—in much the same way that American newspaper readers often find it difficult to understand that culture and history are developing also on other continents beyond the borders of the United States.

All of Europe's weaknesses, nonetheless, must not mislead us into forgetting that Europe remains a strategically important region, indeed decisively important for both the Soviet Union and the West, including the United States. But it may still take a long time for the Europeans to liberate their analytical thoughts from the results of a national differentiation process that has gone on for many centuries—differentiation of languages, of philosophic and religious beliefs, of social and economic fabric, and of political behavior. It will take quite some time, and one must not become prematurely impatient. Do not forget, also, that Americans too have a tendency to be self-centered. Today there is a growing tendency in the United States to focus on its own national interests as it perceives them; at present there prevails almost a kind of euphoria about American vigor and strength, which is reflected in current American arms and military policy. And, frankly, these attitudes are disturbing to Europeans—to some extent their behavior is a reaction to them.

Let me detour now for a parenthetical point. What I had to say about the wish, but present inability, of West Europeans to gain more autonomy vis-à-vis the United States is even truer of the relationship between the Eastern European nations and Moscow. This relationship is a caricature, so to speak, of what I have said about the American-West European relationship.

I can illustrate the situation with one little incident—little in American eyes, little in Soviet eyes, but enormous in European eyes—that happened in the summer and fall of 1982. At that time the Americans and the Russians were negotiating in Geneva about intermediate-range nuclear forces (INF) in Europe. My friend Paul Nitze was the American negotiator. No one in Europe was eager to have additional nuclear missiles on their soil, neither the Poles or Hungarians or Czechs or East Germans—none of the communist regimes—nor the West Germans, the Dutch, the Belgians, the Italians, or even the British. But the deployment of additional missiles hinged on the outcome of these negotiations. We had set aside four years for them, and the United States had promised close consultation at every stage.

Then, in the summer of 1982, Nitze, in the course of a famous "walk in the woods" outside Geneva with his Soviet counterpart, introduced a compromise formula for an INF arms limitation agreement; I would still buy his formula at the drop of a hat, because it was a wise compromise. But without consulting, without even informing, their allies, both Moscow and Nitze's own administration in Washington rejected the compromise. The American public was scarcely aware of the incident, even after it was revealed several months later. But it caused deep dissatisfaction and resentment in West European democratic governments, and a similar reaction was clearly visible among East European communist governments.

As this incident suggests and illustrates, West Europeans are not completely off the track in feeling that they must be on their guard against the political hegemony of the United States. After all, it is primarily Europe's fate that is at stake with the SS-20s. They cannot hit the United States but are aimed at Western Europe, just as American missiles deployed in Western Europe are aimed at targets in East Germany, Poland, Hungary, Czechoslovakia, and Russia. This is something the United States must understand. Moreover, the American obligation to consult closely with its European allies during the INF talks in Geneva was an integral part of the NATO decision of 1979, in accordance with which the INF negotiations were initiated and a number of European countries (with the exception of France) undertook to have American INF missiles deployed eventually on their soil. The total lack of consultation prior to the American rejection of the compromise formula was clearly an act of unwarranted American dominance.

President Reagan's Strategic Defense Initiative was also a heavy blow. There was no allied consultation whatever before Mr. Reagan publicly declared on March 23, 1983, that SDI was meant to "change the course of history" and, by erecting an ultimate leak-proof defense against ballistic missiles, even make strategic nuclear weapons obsolete. He clearly envisaged a reversal of the hitherto agreed-upon strategy of nuclear retaliation and thereby nuclear deterrence.

The idea of defense against an adversary's nuclear missiles was of course not really new; both the United States and the Soviet Union had done research on anti-missile weapons at least since the 1960s, and in 1972, in the ABM Treaty, they had agreed to a strict limit on the number of such weapons systems in order to limit the arms race and maintain equilibrium in mutual deterrence.

Now, after the President's speech, all this was suddenly made to appear obsolete, or that at least was the President's aim. There was also an implication that the French and British nuclear forces would become obsolete in the future. And the announcement seemed to imply a shift of budget emphasis away from conventional defense toward anti-nuclear defense, thereby tending to open even wider the avenue for pressure on Europe from Soviet conventional forces.

Even today, more than two years later, it remains quite unclear whether even a half-satisfactory defense against Soviet strategic missiles can be achieved. It will take another decade to judge whether anything more than some additional defense of American missile sites is attainable. To the European governments, it seems unlikely that their population can be safeguarded by SDI, given the short distances traveled by missiles targeted on Europe, and, in particular, the actual and potential threat from contour-following unmanned bombers, or cruise missiles, against which no SDI would be effective.

Moreover, the Europeans know that the Russians

will not permit themselves to be outproduced. The Russians are concerned about the prospect of weakening their economy, but they will be able to match the pace, possibly with only a little time lag. They will simply make their people suffer a little more in order to use a higher percentage of their GNP for military purposes. But the European governments do not have the slightest interest in economic warfare; they are interested in equilibrium and stability.

For all these reasons, the attempt by the American administration to force the SDI on the alliance has astonished and deeply concerned the allies in Europe. Secretary Weinberger's subsequent urgent invitation to the allies to join the program within sixty days was just the dot on the i.

The United States may get away with this latest exercise in high-handed, unilateral decisionmaking. But the same thing may happen that happened with the 1980 grain embargo and the 1982 pipeline embargo. In both of these cases the Europeans, who had not been consulted, flatly refused to participate, because they do not believe in trade wars and trade wars are not in their interest. Washington had to lift both embargoes shortly after they were imposed.

The absence of leadership in Europe seems to invite American dominance. But too much domineering by people in Washington who have little international experience undermines Europe's confidence in the most important member of the alliance and thereby in the alliance itself.

I repeat, Europe still has unused potential—enormous economic, financial, monetary, industrial, and military potential. It is not being used to the full, primarily because of a lack of leadership within Western Europe itself. The necessary leadership, toward cooperation, could come from a group of nations or from a single country—or from an outstanding individual—for reasons I have already discussed. I have already advised Americans not to be impatient. They should avoid using prematurely such derogatory terms as "Euro-sclerosis."

The United States has a relatively short history, during which it has never seen foreign armies on its soil. Unlike the Russians, the Poles, the Germans, the French, and many others, it has never experienced disastrous defeat or had to make disastrous sacrifices. For these and other reasons, the United States has the greatest vitality of any nation in the world. And, I would like to add, the United States is by far the most generous nation, once its generosity has been called upon. On top of that, Americans are optimists by birth, or at least by education. Sometimes that optimism seems somewhat naive to Europeans, because we have become more or less skeptical as a result of historic experience, but America's optimism is clearly rather helpful in most cases. For all these reasons, I have not only deep-seated sympathy for the American nation but also some understanding of its feeling of superiority from time to time. But if I may offer one little bit of advice: At this moment in history, do not show too openly the superiority you assume you have. Instead take the advice of that wise philosopher who said, "The Athenians do not mind a man being clever as long as he keeps it to himself."

In any event, Americans must not forget that in terms of American Grand Strategy—or, to use Henry Kissinger's phrase, "geostrategy"—Western Europe and its highly educated, very industrious, and ingenious people will remain an indispensable factor in Western strength. Europe will remain indispensable to an America that wants to maintain its own liberty and peace.

3

Problems in Three Regions outside NATO

he interests, as well as the interdependence of interests, of both the United States and the European countries reach much farther than the geographic area of joint defense defined by their NATO treaty. But how far and to what avail can the allied countries pursue their global interests? To what extent can their policies in these areas, sometimes called the Third World, have at least a common thrust and direction? Let me take three different areas as examples in order to examine these questions.

The Latin American Debt Problem

Since the United States became the only Western world power, as one of the consequences of World War II, it has discovered that it is strategically a two-ocean power. Nevertheless it took the wars in Korea and Vietnam, plus the successful economic development of Japan and a few other East Asian nations over the last fifteen years, to make Americans generally understand to the full the Pacific dimension in their Grand Strategy and worldview. And in spite of the Monroe Doctrine, the war with Spain at the end of the last century, and the Cuban missile crisis in 1962, it has taken the United States almost until today to understand that it is a three-ocean power—

deeply and inextricably involved in the geographic area around and across the Gulf of Mexico and the Caribbean Sea.

This involvement extends not only to Mexico, Cuba, Nicaragua, El Salvador, the Isthmus land bridge that links the Americas, and the Caribbean Basin, but, as I perceive it, to all the 400 million present inhabitants of Latin America, who early in the next century are bound to have increased to close to the 700-million mark. Already today, and even more emphatically then, Latin America is and will be the largest concentration of Catholics on the globe as well as the largest concentration of people speaking one European language (to be precise, with the Brazilians speaking Portuguese, two closely related European languages). Although most of these countries were liberated from European colonial imperialism early in the last century, thanks to the Libertador, Simon Bolivar, and others, they have nevertheless, over several generations, fallen under the class rule of rather small oligarchies. Since Christopher Columbus's time, millions have been kept backward and illiterate, and most of them have been exploited. Whenever any of the people tried to liberate themselves during the nineteenth and twentieth centuries, dictatorships or military governments were set up to keep the country quiet and let the economy run smoothly. These economies were mainly coastal economies, with great stretches of backward areas in the hinterland.

This state of affairs suited Latin America's trading partners in Europe and North America well. Only in recent years have a number of these countries begun the transition from authoritarian rule to pluralism or democracy—Argentina, Brazil, and Peru are examples—but because of misery and unrest the movements toward democracy are now in danger. The misery and unrest invite foreign interference, either clandestinely through communist infiltration or Cuban-Soviet arms transfers or openly through North American not-so-covert action, military threats, and the like.

The pervasive instability of the area clearly has worldwide strategic implications. Watching the unfolding drama with great unease are the United States, the Roman Catholic Church, the European states—Spain and Italy in particular—and the private banks of the Western world, as well as the Soviet Union. But so far neither the West as a whole nor the United States has developed a Grand Strategy for Latin America—one that must, first of all, help the Latin Americans define and find their own destiny reflecting their own historic heritage, their religious belief, and their desire for freedom and economic well-being.

The second major objective of such a Grand Strategy should be to assure coherent and expanding economic links between this large continent and the free world economy as a whole. In the short run this means dealing, step by step, with the present Latin American debt problem and also the dangers it poses to great banks in Wall Street, London, and Frankfurt and ultimately to the whole banking and credit system on which the free world depends.

And a Grand Strategy is needed, thirdly, that will eliminate the danger of Soviet intervention, direct or by proxy, and thereby also eliminate the possibility of war. A war in that region might not necessarily be as geographically limitable as the recent conflicts in the Falklands/Malvinas and Grenada. It could very well lead to something quite big.

To understand the present economic mess in Latin America, one has to look back over the last decade or so. When the two oil price explosions took place in 1973–74 and 1979–80, many of the non-oil-producing countries in South America that had come to enjoy marked economic progress and growth faced a serious dilemma. Most of them had to buy oil abroad: Brazil, for example, did not have a drop of oil, nor did it have any coal either. But they had to pay for their oil imports in dollars, and from 1972 to the present the dollar price of oil has risen twentyfold. And whereas they have always earned hard currency by selling their coffee and sugar and bananas, the price for these commodities has only doubled during the last twenty years, and no one wants to consume more sugar or coffee. We are not drinking twenty times as much coffee today or putting twenty-five times as much sugar in our coffee.

So, because of the oil price explosion, these countries have been unable to earn enough money from their exports to pay for their oil. Therefore, they have had to borrow hard currency to finance the large deficits in their balance of trade. At the same time, after the first oil price shock, there was plenty of dollar liquidity to finance loans, because enormous dollar surpluses accumulated in a number of OPEC countries. The Western banking system and the Western governments then invented what was called the "recycling of petrodollars."

This sounded nice and was for some time benevolent and constructive. The Arab and other OPEC countries placed most of their surplus dollars in short-term deposits in Western banks. The Western banks then made short-term credits available to Brazil, Argentina, and the other Latin American countries. But the banks and governments alike failed to realize that, although the credits were extended on a short-term basis, in fact they became long-term. When they could not be repaid after three months, they had to be rolled over and new additional credit extended for the next three months, and then after the next three months they had to be rolled over again and new credit extended again for the third three months. For all practical purposes, they became long-term credits, and with every rollover the interest rates grew and grew and grew because of the rise in interest rates in the United States.

In August 1982, Mexico became the first country unable to make payments that were due, and the Mexican government learned the truth of Mark Twain's statement that "A banker is a fellow who lends you his umbrella when the sun is shining and wants it back the minute it begins to rain." Not only did Mexico learn it but so did all the others, including governments in East Europe and Africa. And the Western bankers discovered that the debtors were not able to give the umbrella back, that is, make payments on the principal. They were not even able to pay all the interest. Only then did the world realize that it was facing a general debt crisis that was not limited to Latin America, though it was concentrated there.

The situation became still more serious when OPEC stopped accumulating petrodollars. In 1983–84 Saudi Arabia even drew about $30 billion from its deposits abroad in order to finance the later stages of big domestic programs undertaken soon after the first oil price explosion, which had made them seem very, very rich. It could not accumulate more petrodollars, because the price of oil stopped rising; on the contrary, it has declined over the last two years because of the worldwide depression and because people all over the world have used less oil and have therefore imported less. With a smaller global demand for oil, the price has not gone up but has dropped. So we have come to the end of the petrodollar saga.

Budgetary, monetary, and altogether inflationary policies within Latin America, plus the flight of a substantial amount of capital to Western industrialized countries, did the rest to bring about the mess in Latin America. Some of the governments then proceeded to put their economies in a severe domestic squeeze. Smaller budgets, less investment in fixed capital, slower growth, greater unemployment, and even famine were the inevitable consequences of austerity programs. One Latin American president said to me two years ago, "I will shortly have to decide whether it is more important for me to pay interest to some banks abroad or to feed my own people." It was a serious remark. Of course it was also a short-sighted remark, because if he stopped paying interest he would never be able to acquire the new credits he would need to buy imports to feed his growing nation in the future. For this reason, he has chosen to squeeze his economy in order to pay interest. The decision also benefits quite a few banks in Frankfurt, London, and particularly New York City, which might collapse if they no longer received interest payments, because, especially in the United States, they have to write off or sharply revalue their outstanding loan assets if they do not receive interest payments over a period longer than ninety days. They would have to write off loans that totaled more than their entire assets.

To sum this up, there were four reasons for the economic mess in Latin America: first, the oil price explosions; second, the enormous increase in dollar interest rates; third, the irresponsible acceleration of borrowing from foreign private banks; and fourth, the irresponsible lending by almost all of our private banks, which were not prudently enough controlled by our central banks, our regulatory authorities, the International Monetary Fund, or the governments of Western Europe and North America.

Since the low point of 1982–83, we have, to be sure, witnessed considerable progress in the management of the crisis. The external deficits of several key debtor countries have contracted markedly and turned partly into trade surpluses—at first because of austerity policies that reduced imports, more recently because of an expansion of exports to meet the large demand created in the United States by its budget deficits. The increase in overall debt has slowed, and massive amounts of public and private debt have been rescheduled, primarily as a result of the diligence and foresight of the International Monetary Fund and its general manager, M. Jacques de Larosière, as well as the cooperation of private lender banks.

All of this is an extraordinary achievement. Yet, and here I borrow a sentence from Henry Kissinger, "I have the impression that the current system of debt management is reaching its inherent limit." The rescheduling agreements have to be reopened and renegotiated every twelve months. Terms that were agreed upon in good faith yesterday have to be renegotiated today. Some lender banks have gone as far as profit-making institutions can. The necessity to renegotiate and the volatility of interest rates have produced a situation in which no finance minister in a Latin American country can really calculate how much, in hard currency, his country will have to transfer to the foreign lender banks during the next twelve months—and certainly not beyond that time.

The economic adjustments required by the International Monetary Fund are quite reasonable, but they do not necessarily take into account the domestic political situations in the debtor countries. Austerity measures that are too harsh invite trouble, and trouble is an invitation to the military to seize power again.

As we in the creditor countries look at this situation, we must recognize that it was the fundamental worldwide economic upheaval, in the first place, and to some degree our own mistakes that led to the condition of excessive indebtedness. It was not just the fault of the Latin Americans. It would be unfair, as well as profoundly unwise, to try to make them bear the brunt of the problem.

Yet today, with respect to this problem, the United States and Western Europe are conducting their economic policies almost exclusively in their own domestic context, as a serious problem for their banks and their credit systems but not something much bigger. Most of the American public still views the United States as relatively unaffected by international economic developments; the American political process has not yet adjusted to the reality that the United States has become deeply integrated into the world economy and especially into the fabric of international finance.

The present situation was, I think, aptly described by Anatole Kaletsky in the London *Financial Times:*

Can a policy which requires relatively poor countries like Brazil, Mexico, and Argentina to generate huge trade surpluses year after year until the end of the century, can it be described as a permanent and sustainable solution to the debt problem? Between 1983 and 1992 Brazil's trade surpluses will have to average 4% of GNP and Mexico's will have to average 7% every year if they are to meet their interest payments with little or no extra additional borrowing.

It is, of course, almost impossible to achieve such high figures on a permanent basis. They are larger trade surpluses than even Japan has succeeded in earning; the Japanese trade surplus was less than 3 percent of the Japanese GNP last year. How can Brazil or Mexico do better? They obviously cannot. Kaletsky went on to say:

If a downturn in world economic growth or any upsurge of protectionism in the United States and in other industrialized countries should coincide with a need in Latin America to redirect more resources toward domestic consumption then the world would soon face another crisis.

I think this judgment is absolutely correct.

It seems to me essential that all the governments involved should now agree on an economic strategy; it would have to ask for sacrifices on almost every side. The debtor countries should seek early advice from the International Monetary Fund and pursue programs agreed upon with the Fund. But realistic adjustment programs must combine a sustained improvement in their balance of payments with a resumption of economic growth. In order to bring this about, the debtor countries should try to attract more direct private investment from abroad and create conditions favorable to the return of capital that has fled the country.

However, it is politically intolerable for the debtor countries not to know the maximum debt service, in dollars, that they will be responsible for during the next twelve months. They need some degree of protection by the IMF against fluctuating interest rates. The essential, even if unpopular, role of the IMF must continue to be to negotiate adjustment programs for those countries confronting balance-of-payment or debt-servicing problems. Of course there must be conditions, or new credit will not be made available.

It is sad that the IMF has been made to appear a kind of devil by countries all over the world. In this regard, the developing countries are wrong. It reminds me of the ancient Hebrews, who had a goat on which all the sins were placed. The scapegoat principle is neither new nor helpful. It will not help the developing countries of Latin America to hold the IMF responsible for their mess and thereby make the IMF ineffective. They would simply not get any more credit, because private banks lend fresh money only to the extent that the IMF has negotiated a viable economic environment. An element of austerity is therefore inevitable. But the IMF should not push austerity beyond the point absolutely essential for successful medium-term adjustment of these economies. To go beyond that would be, in most cases, self-defeating.

The coordinated approach I have just outlined would be a considerable improvement over the present uncertain policy situation in both the creditor and debtor countries. But in all probability even this degree of change does not go far enough. It may be that the West as a whole should consider a new concept. I would call it a "General Agreement to Lend," borrowing the label in part from the existing General Agreement to Borrow that goes back to the early days of the Bretton Woods system and the IMF.

The essence of such a General Agreement to Lend would be an undertaking by major creditor governments to support a reorganization of the debt structures that would reduce the load on the debtor countries at least until they could dig themselves out. It might include a consolidation of short-term debt into medium-term fixed-interest bonds to replace the present multiyear rescheduling, and it might also restrict debt service transfers to an agreed-upon maximum percentage of the export earnings of the debtor country. The new General Agreement might even embrace some capitalization of interest. To the extent that all this reduced the burden on the debtor countries, the slack would be taken up primarily by funds contributed on an agreed basis by the creditor countries.

The private creditor banks have to contribute something. Not only do they have to provide fresh money; they also have to provide interest relief in cases where debtor countries are making a good faith commitment to carry out the programs they have agreed upon with the IMF; the banks also have to agree to mechanisms that will cap the debt service transfers the debtor countries have to make.

It is easy to draw up such a list of actions, much more difficult to make governments understand its necessity. To some extent the European governments understand the necessity better than Wall Street, but so far the Europeans have chosen to let the IMF and Wall Street occupy center stage. The Europeans—and this is true of governments as well as of commercial banks—are more or less hanging back. So is the American government.

Central America

European governments, I am convinced, often understand the domestic political problems of Latin American countries somewhat better than Washington does. This may be in part because these problems have more in common with events in European history than with anything in the North American past. But more than this it is the result of a built-in bias that affects American judgment: traditionally (and rather naturally), the United States has tended, with rare exceptions, to take the side of those governments in Latin America that defend American property and American economic interests and stress law and order. More than once there has been U.S. military intervention to help save such governments from defeat. This has provoked anti-Yankee emotions in quite a few Latin American countries, of course, particularly in the Caribbean Basin. In the perception of many people in Central America, the model of American capitalism stands largely for economic exploitation and dependence. This has made Marxism attractive to quite a few.

The future development of Central America depends to a large extent, it seems to me, on how the United States acts with respect to necessary economic, social, and political change in that region. The United States, of course, has vital interests there, whereas the Soviet Union does not. But from a global political point of view and an ideological point of view, the Soviets are interested in having the United States tied up in the Central American theater. It suits Soviet interests to divert worldwide attention from Soviet power politics—in Afghanistan, for example. It may be in the Soviet interest some day in the future to exploit anti-American feeling in Central America and thus create disturbances in the relationship between the United States and Europe. The Soviets hope to take advantage of a deterioration of the situation in order to export communism, interfere with domestic development within the Central American countries, and gain political influence.

It seems axiomatic that peace and economic progress can be achieved in that region only if the co-operation of the United States is sought. Nothing will be accomplished against the will of the United States. But the ideas for solutions will have to come from the region itself.

Thus, European opinion today focuses on support for the initiative of the five nations in and bordering on Central America known as the Contadora group. The Contadora process has developed slowly in the past three years, but the proposals developed through it are promising. Whatever its shortcomings, there seems to be no visible alternative to pursuing it with more vigor than the United States has shown most of the time.

West Europeans have a clear interest in peaceful solutions in Central America. If the problems cannot be solved peacefully, then, in the European percep-tion, the danger might arise that the traditionally good and close relations between Europe and Latin America might be jeopardized. The credibility of the United States as the Western leader might also be damaged in the eyes of a considerable part of the Western European public, and this would add a strain to the European-American relationship. The Euro-peans also fear that war in Central America, which is not entirely unthinkable, might lead to horizontal escalation—triggering Soviet or Cuban responses or retaliation in other parts of the world.

In the present, rather tense, phase of political de-velopment in Central America, no external interfer-ence should be permitted—either by Cuba or by the

Soviet Union. But limiting ourselves to a purely military strategy would be anachronistic: in the long run, the dangers within Central America cannot be eliminated by power politics or by military might. What is needed instead is a positive long-range economic strategy to improve the sad situation of the majority of the people.

This is especially true of Central America, but it is also true of Latin America as a whole. Let us look at the simplest yardstick: Costa Rica, El Salvador, Guatemala, Honduras, and Nicaragua—all of them together—have today an aggregate gross national product that is less than 1 percent of the GNP of the United States and only a little larger than 1 percent of that of Western Europe. It is less than $30 billion, as compared to a gross national product of more than $3 trillion in the United States and $2 trillion in the European Economic Community. To improve the economic situation of these five countries is obviously within our own economic reach. A Reagan Plan to double their per capita GNP in real terms within seven or ten years is easily conceivable.

The reluctant response of the U.S. public and Congress to the economic aid recommendations of the Kissinger Commission suggest no great enthusiasm for such a project, although a limited start has been made, essentially on a U.S.-only basis. But would it not add a new and important dimension if Europe were asked to participate in a truly joint program? I am certain that the European governments would be overwhelmingly more enthusiastic about giving financial assistance to such a plan for Central America than about accepting the current American invitation to pool their budgets in space-war research. A joint Marshall Plan, or Reagan Plan, for Central America financed by the United States, Canada, and the Europeans would also have the beneficial side effect of removing the everpresent suspicion of the Latin Americans that the United States seeks power and domination in the region for its own sake.

Before leaving this subject, I would like to add a word concerning the role of the Catholic Church in Latin America, particularly in Central America. I understand full well the Holy Father sticking to a rather conservative theology, which I do not criticize here; I am not a Catholic myself. I also understand his fight against the so-called theology of liberation, or theology of revolution. But this is only the negative half of what is needed. The positive half, which the Catholic Church could come up with, should be to develop a social teaching, as the Catholic Church did over a period of almost a hundred years in Central Europe. Seeing the misery of industrial workers in the 1880s and 1890s, the Holy See published its great social encyclical *Rerum Novarum*, and again, forty years later at the beginning of the world economic depression, the great encyclical *Quadragesimo Anno*. These and other social and economic teachings of the Catholic Church have had great impact on the development of a sound social and economic structure in Europe during the last ninety years.

In the light of this tradition, it would be appropriate if the bishops of South America—as well as the bishops of North America and Europe—and the Bishop of Rome would together convene all their experts in order to study the complexities of the situation (and not limit themselves to worrying about the misery!). If they are entitled to teach the world about peace in the nuclear age, they are even more entitled to offer fresh ideas about what could and should be done to secure human dignity in Latin America from a Christian point of view and to teach governments to adopt a Christian attitude toward their neighbors in Latin America. It is just not enough—it is self-defeating—if in practical terms they confine themselves to fighting against contraception and thereby fostering the population explosion.

The Middle East

The economic situation of the world in recent years has been called a recession by some Americans, but for most people it has been a depression. The economic depression since the two oil shocks has reminded us that almost all of Europe (except England and Norway), Japan, and many other countries are largely dependent on oil coming from the Persian Gulf and the Middle East. For that reason alone, though also for several other reasons, it is of the utmost strategic importance to maintain peace in that region. The United States, Canada, Venezuela,

Mexico, China, the Soviet Union, all have oil within their own borders, and some have natural gas and coal as well. But the Japanese and the Europeans, and most Latin Americans, Africans, and Asians, have no oil at all. They depend on the unimpeded import of oil, on unimpeded production in the Middle East, on free and continuous sea transport, and, in addition to sufficient quantities of oil, on reasonable international prices. So does the United States to a large extent. It was the 1973 war between Israel and its neighbors that triggered OPEC's first oil shock. It is therefore understandable that Japanese and Europeans and many Americans think of their oil supplies first when they hear bad news from the Middle East.

It is also understandable that most Americans and Europeans think first of the fate of Israel and Egypt, Jordan, Syria, and Lebanon. Some industrialists in the Western world hope for additional weapons sales. Some bankers think first of the deposits of their Arab clients. The staffs in the foreign and defense ministries in the West, as well as in the East, think of the Middle East as a region of the world where the future is particularly difficult to predict but where developments could easily cause a change in the global balance of power. And these serious officials and makers of policy—in contrast to most of the general public—know that the region is not characterized by just one conflict (around Israel) but presents an almost incomprehensible complex of conflicts, riddles, and enigmas.

Going from the outer ranges of the area to the

center, start with the tensions between India, with its Hindu majority, and Islamic Pakistan—India now having developed nuclear devices that could be converted to military use, with Pakistan not far behind. India leans toward Pakistan's northern neighbor, which is the Soviet Union; in turn, Pakistan leans toward India's eastern neighbor, which is the People's Republic of China.

And wedged among all four is Afghanistan, which has been suffering under Russian occupation since the end of 1979. The Soviets are following the old line of expansion the Tsars tried in the last century in order to bring Afghanistan under their control or influence. They have now built a number of modern airfields in Afghanistan that are rather close to the Persian Gulf, that is, to Kuwait, the Emirates, Saudi Arabia, and so on. Obviously they are slowly and prudently reaching for ports in the warm waters of the Persian Gulf or the Indian Ocean. They already have a military and political presence in several spots in that oil region of the world. They once had a stronghold in Egypt, until Anwar Sadat threw them out in 1972, but then they popped up in a stronger position in other countries, Syria for example. They are also present in South Yemen, formerly called Aden, at the southern tip of the Arabian peninsula. They are present in Ethiopia. They also have good connections with Colonel Qaddafi in Libya.

The United States too maintains a military and political presence in the area. There is some political cooperation with the Saudis, a great deal more, including economic cooperation, with Egypt. The United States has a strategic understanding with Israel, which means to the rest of the people of the area that the United States is not an impartial power. For some Arabs, this situation rules out any possibility that the Americans can bring about peace in the region.

Then, of course, there is the perennial conflict between Israel and its immediate Arab neighbors—Syria, Lebanon, Jordan, and Egypt. The peace treaty between Israel and Egypt, brought about by Sadat and the Camp David meetings of 1978 and 1979, left out Syria, Lebanon, and Jordan. It left unsettled the complex problems of the Israeli-occupied West Bank of the Jordan River, which up to 1967 was governed as part of the state of Jordan. It also left unsettled the complex problems of Jerusalem, which contains the holy places of the three great monotheistic religions of the world.

For these reasons, one observes a verbal accord among all the Arab states within the Arab League (Egypt was ushered out after Camp David but is now hoping to be readmitted). There is verbal solidarity with the Palestine Liberation Organization and Arafat. The fact that Jerusalem is the third most important holy place in the world for Muslims after Mecca and Medina means that there is in the Arab League at least a strong common bond of religious concern for the city and the area.

And then there is the pressure of the Palestinian refugees, living now in most of the other Arab countries; they are intelligent, literate people, many of whom have worked their way up in the bureaucracies of Saudi Arabia and other Arab countries and now have some inside leverage. In some of the conservative Arab states the presence of these refugees inside their own bureaucracies and economies gives rise to a lot of anxiety. So, even more, does Muslim fundamentalism, whether its present surge was first instigated by the Ayatollah Khomeini on the Shi'ite side or later on also came from the Sunni side of Islam. Iran's potential for ideological expansion is a great worry, and there is also, of course, considerable concern about Russia. Yet even this formidable catalogue is far from a full picture of the tensions in the Middle East.

The war between Iran and Iraq, both oil suppliers, endangers the transport of oil from the gulf. Syria and Israel have interests at stake in the Iran-Iraq war and are clandestinely intervening, but they are not the only ones. In northern Iraq the Kurds are fighting for their freedom; some live in Iraq, some in Iran, some in the Soviet Union, and some in Turkey. They are one people split among four different countries, and they want to get together. No one can control events in that small (relatively speaking) area of conflict around Iraq. But it is just one area of conflict among two dozen!

Nor can anyone control the political behavior of Qaddafi, who sees himself as the leader of the rejection front, of states that opposed and vilified Camp

David. Libya has only a few inhabitants, but it can still dispose of large amounts of oil-surplus dollars, which Qaddafi uses to promote Arab nationalism and Muslim fundamentalism everywhere in the Middle East. He made Nimeiri's position in the Sudan untenable, he interfered in Chad, and he threatens to infiltrate Egypt.

The most populous of all the Arab states, Egypt under Nasser was the leading power within the Arab League. Al-Azhar University in Cairo is still the educational center of Islam; its spiritual influence reaches even into the Islamic republics of the Soviet Union and eastward into Indonesia and the Philippines. Sadat's great peace initiative recovered the Sinai Peninsula; it also forced Egypt to step down as leader of the Arab world. Sadat, for whom I felt deep friendship, was a man who had a profound religious belief in the necessity and possibility of peace. He was less an Arab than Nasser and more an Egyptian. His assassination points to the danger that is on the minds of all "moderate" Arab leaders, including the Arab mayors of the cities in the West Bank, who need to and are willing to cooperate to some extent with the Israeli military government. Egypt faces huge economic problems, aggravated by increasing overpopulation. All of its water comes from the Sudan, so Sudan's political attitude is of greatest importance to Hosni Mubarak in Cairo. He does not seek Arab leadership—he is a modest man—but he does strive to reestablish normal diplomatic relations with the Arab states. His recent meeting with Yassir Arafat of the PLO should be seen in this context.

For the same reason, that is, to legitimate their negotiations with Israel and Shimon Peres, King Hussein of Jordan and Arab leaders on the West Bank seem to need the PLO and Arafat; they put up with the added prestige Arafat may gain from the association. Only Assad's Syria can afford to fight Arafat, because Assad feels no need to conclude any negotiations with Israel. Syria is by no means a puppet of the Soviet Union, but it is confident that it will always get enough Soviet assistance to prevent its being overrun by Israel. Assad feels strong enough to try to impose indirect Syrian control over Lebanon. He will try as well to attain Arab leadership. But he does not have oil; he is poor. Not only is he incomparably poorer than King Fahd of Saudi Arabia, but his resources do not permit him to match the well-financed diplomacy of Qaddafi. As for Saudi Arabia, it will not commit itself to any one Arab country; they are very cautious in Riyadh.

Almost all of the states in the Middle East have vulnerable political regimes. We are reminded of this by the assassinations of Indira Gandhi and Anwar Sadat, by the execution of a Pakistani president and of an Iranian prime minister, and by endless acts of terrorism almost everywhere. The outstanding example of course is Lebanon. Indeed, one cannot speak of a political regime in Lebanon. There are six large religious groups and seventeen officially recognized sects. They play power politics and fight a civil war against each other, some backed by Syria, some backed by Iran, some backed by Israel or by the West. But on top of that, there are in Lebanon regular Syrian troops, plus United Nations teams, and, finally, many thousands of Palestinians. Three years of Israeli warfare inside Lebanon have not solved a single problem; the same was true of the temporary American military presence.

In comparison, the situation in nearby Cyprus seems much simpler, with only two major adversaries, the Greeks and the Turks, confronting each other. Although both are members of the North Atlantic alliance, so far the alliance has been totally unable to ease the tension or bring about a modus vivendi. In fact, the tension between Ankara and Athens has considerably weakened the southern flank of NATO.

I have not tried to give a complete picture of the situation in the Middle East, only to give enough examples to illustrate the complexities of the region. In my view there is no chance that the West, or the United States, can bring about a "solution" for this troubled region that could possibly achieve a stabilized peace. Only a utopian idealist could suppose that this is possible.

If the Soviet Union is driven out of one country, it will pop up in another; no one can prevent this from happening. In general, the Arabs would rather rely on America than on the Soviet Union, but they are disappointed by what they see as the United

States' pro-Israeli policies. And many are prepared to deal with the Russians: the farther an Arab country is from the Soviet Union, the more willing it is to accept Soviet aid, which means Soviet military hardware and Soviet military advisers.

No American leader and no Soviet leader—and no European leader either—should imagine for a moment that he or she has a solution to the problems between Israelis and Arabs or the tensions between the oil-rich, conservative Arab countries and the radical movements and regimes. It is no wonder to me that U.S. policies have changed more often in the Middle East than in any other region of the world, because none of these policies was ever about to lead to lasting success. Moscow's policies have been more cautious. The Soviets have been content just to have a thumb in the pie.

The Europeans have been a little wiser so far; they have more or less followed a policy of noninterference. They have maintained normal diplomatic and trade relations with all the states in the region, never ostracizing any one country. Nor have they ostracized the Organization of Petroleum Exporting Countries, or any subgrouping of OPEC's members (I might mention here that two European countries, the United Kingdom and Norway, as undeclared but honorary members of OPEC, have profited quite a bit, until very recently, from OPEC's pricing policies). The Europeans know full well that they cannot defend their sources of oil around the Persian Gulf in any war that might break out. The best they can do, together with the United States, is to attempt strictly limited operations, such as sending French or Italian or British peacekeeping forces to Lebanon.

The truth is that no one in the world can defend the Persian Gulf oil. If some madman, or terrorist group, or one of the two countries at war right now in the northern tip of the gulf—Iran and Iraq—should choose to, it could set fire to and blow up the oilfields around the gulf. Nor can any one defend the world against the economic consequences of such an event. The best we can do is to try from time to time to shift our weight a little bit to one side or the other of a particular conflict, in order to maintain the balance in the conflict and to try to prevent brush fires from becoming big fires. There may even be times when the West has to do this together with the Soviet Union.

The idealistic American perception that an American Grand Strategy for the Middle East can solve its complex problems and bring about a just and stable peace seems unrealistic and outdated to me. It reminds me of John Galsworthy's remark that "Idealism increases in direct proportion to one's distance from the problem." Lasting peace was achieved in that region most recently by the Ottoman Empire, which maintained rigid regimes and placed soldiers everywhere. The United States cannot do that today. In spite of all its intercontinental strategic power to destroy, it cannot do that. It could not even rescue the American hostages from Teheran by the kind of limited conventional military operation the Israelis used to liberate people from a hijacked aircraft in Entebbe and the Germans used, under rather more advantageous circumstances, to rescue a hijacked aircraft in Somalia.

The best one can hope for is to defuse explosive situations on a case-by-case basis, stop wars, and otherwise carry on the diligent psychological diplomacy that Americans—Henry Kissinger, among others—have carried on in the Middle East for a long time. To hope for more would be futile. But of course diligent diplomacy does need a certain amount of cooperation between the Americans and those European powers that have traditionally had influence in the Middle East, namely, Britain, France, to a surprising extent Spain, and also some other European countries.

The Russians also have influence there, whether we like it or not. They too are afraid of war in the Persian Gulf region. They want to expand their influence gradually, step by step. That makes containment, as well as restraint, necessary on the Western side. We can assume that the results of a major war in the Middle East would be as incalculable for them as they would be for us.

The Far East

I have recently spent some time in the People's Republic of China. My impression is that the Chinese are, in the main, busy implementing the general economic reforms they have drawn up. After five or six years of successful experimentation in the field of agriculture, they are now extending the thrust of these reforms to the more difficult problems of the cities and urban industries.

They do have strategic worries. They are somewhat concerned about the Soviet Union—about the SS-20s in Asia, the growth of the Soviet Pacific fleet, and Soviet bases in Vietnam, at Da Nang and Cam Ranh Bay. Of course they are also concerned about Afghanistan and about the Soviet Union permitting Vietnam to conquer Laos and Cambodia. They hope that Russia's attention is occupied by Western Europe, the United States, and the Atlantic alliance. And they are a bit concerned that the United States may not be strong enough in the Pacific and the entire Far East in the future.

Despite these external concerns, they have given priority to developing their industry, their scientific research, and their education. The army will come only fourth, which, by the way, is one of several difficulties they have to overcome during the period of reform. The revolution definitely is over. What we see now in China is an era of reform. Or, to be more cautious, whether it becomes an era of reform will depend on how long Deng Xiaoping can carry on physically and how long he can master situations as they occur. The Chinese will try to follow a strategy of equidistance from Washington as much as from Moscow. From time to time they will show Washington their Russian card, and from time to

time they will show Moscow their American card.
But one can be certain the strategy will be one of
equidistance.

To help carry out their economic plans, they will
open China up to the world economy; they are already in the process of opening up to the world markets, including the financial markets. China is the
only large nation in the world that has not yet been
touched by the world's economic disorder. Why? Because it has not been entangled in the world's economic fabric. But now they are starting to change
that, which will bring some risks but at the same
time make it possible for them to acquire quickly
the benefit of Western managerial knowledge, Western technological skill, Western investment goods,
and so on.

The principal beneficiary of China's entry into
world markets will be Japan. Japan needs oil, and in
a couple of years China will be able to export oil to
Japan, and coal as well. To import technology from
Japan does not make the Chinese uneasy. They would
much rather import technology from Japan than from
the United States and thereby become somewhat
dependent on a superpower. They might even prefer
Europe or Germany to the United States as a source
of technology and capital goods.

The Chinese do not have friends in their region.
China is just too big, and in past centuries it has not
behaved too nicely toward smaller countries. Only
North Korea is to some extent a friend, but North
Korea has to be cautious, as it too has a common

border with the Russians. Otherwise there are tensions between Beijing and all the neighboring communist governments—the Soviet Union, Mongolia, Vietnam, and the puppet regimes in Cambodia and Laos. It is paradoxical that China has good relations with the capitalist West and rather poor, if not tense, relations with its communist comrades.

China is a developing country; its GNP is around $300 a year per capita. But there are hundreds of millions of Asians in other countries—in South Asia especially—where the standard of living is below the threshold of $200 a year per capita. It is one of those great mystifications that people in the United States believe the world is in good shape economically; it certainly is not. There is greater misery today than there was ten years ago. Of course the economic development of the Asian countries differs very much from country to country. A few are very successful; most are very poor.

China may be on the road to enormous success over the next fifteen years. It depends on whether they can avoid falling into such serious mistakes as a "cultural revolution" or a "great leap forward" or whatever other nonsense they undertook in the last twenty-five years. I have great sympathy for what they are doing today; in my judgment we all have an interest in their success. The stronger they are economically, the more the Russians have to look over their shoulders in the East. And they do. One can expect that Gorbachev will try a new style and make some friendly noises toward Beijing. One can conceive as well of some friendly noises from Beijing, but it will then be important to remember that this is just playing around with the Russian card. It will be played in order to make people in Washington understand that the United States should not overdo its military assistance to Taiwan, for example.

I will not forget the great festival on the first of October 1984 celebrating the thirty-fifth anniversary of the founding of the People's Republic of China. As commander-in-chief, Deng Xiaoping reviewed a huge military parade. He made a speech from high up on the gate that leads from Tian An Men Square into the former Forbidden City. It was a very short speech—just eight minutes—very military in tone and attitude. The last couple of sentences ran like this: "We have just concluded an agreement with the British government on Hong Kong. Every Chinese in Hong Kong can be satisfied with that agreement and proud of it.... Every Chinese living abroad can be satisfied and proud." (This was of course addressed to the Chinese in Taiwan and to the sixteen or seventeen million Chinese living in other Asian countries.) And in conclusion he said: "Every descendant of the yellow emperor can be proud of it." To hear this from the mouth of a communist leader was quite an experience. "Every descendant of the yellow emperor"! It showed the enormous self-confidence that prevails in Beijing now.

I hope they will be successful. They are a developing country; they perceive China as a developing country. They will, at least verbally, become the

major spokesmen for the developing world in the
United Nations and elsewhere. But, practically
speaking, what they are looking for is economic cooperation with the industrialized part of the world.
By the turn of the century, they will have become
the third world power, though not necessarily a superpower, which, by the way, is a word they abhor.
In their understanding, the word "superpower" is
meant for the United States and the Soviet Union as
powers that impose their will on others. The Chinese
leaders say they are not going to do that. And I guess
they will not have a chance to do it for at least the
next fifteen years. What happens in the next century
remains to be seen. They will become world power
number three; they are a nuclear world power already and can destroy Washington and New York
City as well as Moscow or any other place on earth.

As we approach the end of this century, I think
we might as well prepare ourselves for a change from
a bipolar (Moscow and Washington) to a triangular
power situation. It would be wise for us in the West
to accept the rise of China and to do so for the very
same reasons that led Richard Nixon, who was a
good strategist (what he did domestically is not for
me to judge), to open up the China policies of the
United States soon after he came into office. It would
be wise to assist the rise of China economically and
technologically. It would also be wise to be very
careful in assisting Taiwan. Both Chinas are, after
all, dictatorships. One has 1.1 billion people, the other
about 20 million.

Finally, let us consider briefly the other nations in the Far East, Japan in particular. Here my first point concerns Japan's defense budget and military posture. I have already noted that one of the real secrets of Japan's economic success is that it spends only 1 percent of its GNP annually for defense, whereas the United States spends about 7 percent and Europe about 4 percent. The temptation is natural for Americans, faced with this situation and with intense Japanese competition and import penetration, to think in terms of pressuring Japan to raise its defense effort to a major rearmament program.

But I am convinced that any such substantial increase, especially under American pressure, would be profoundly unwise. Everyone in the region would oppose it, including the People's Republic of China. It would be a way to drive China back into a wrong direction. In a way, the Japanese situation is similar to that of the Chinese. The Japanese too have no friends in the region. The memory of Japanese imperialism is still very vivid in the Philippines, in Korea, in China, in Indonesia, in Thailand, in Singapore, and in Malaysia. Japan relies on the United States for its security—it *has* to rely on the United States, because it can neither find alliance partners nor, under General MacArthur's constitution, provide sufficient military forces of its own. Though Japan can and should do a bit more to protect the sea lanes around its territory, it should not be asked to go further.

South Korea also has no friend in the area. And

there is no love lost on either side between the Koreans and the Japanese. South Korea also has to depend on the power of the United States for its defense, therefore, as does Taiwan.

The economic situation in the Far East seems to be distinguished by the progress in Japan, South Korea, Taiwan, Singapore, and Hong Kong. But they might be hit by the world recession after a time lag, so their success must not be exaggerated. The exports of Japan, a nation of 125 million people, are still a little smaller than the exports of Germany, a nation of 60 million. I mention this to correct the mistaken statistical image of Japan's trade that American newspapers convey. But their trade surplus is real. The Japanese would be very wise to use this large trade surplus to increase their development aid, especially in Asia, and make the friends in their region which they lack. Their development aid has so far been very small in terms of their GNP—almost as small as American development aid, which is among the smallest in the world. It might also be wise for the Japanese, instead of putting so much of their production into exports—so that their trade surplus is 3 percent of GNP—to devote much more of their effort to their own domestic needs. Housing especially needs much greater emphasis; it is the only field in which Japan lags behind modern standards of living in the industrialized world.

Be that as it may, it would be wise for all of us in the West to draw Japan as closely into the Western fold as Tokyo is willing to go. This is why France and Germany, in proposing the so-called economic summit meetings ten years ago, considered it essential to have Japan participate from the beginning. It is in our common interest to regard Japan as an integral component of the West's economic and political framework and not to reject it. This is one reason, among others, why it would be very unwise to launch a trade war against Japan and alienate this very important Far Eastern nation. The burdens of the United States in the Far East are already very heavy. They cannot be lightened by either the Europeans or the Japanese. It would be a major strategic mistake to push Japan into tensions with the West or with its neighbors.

W

A Tentative Summary

hether we are considering the Middle East, Latin America (particularly Central America), or the Far East, certain basic observations apply, though in varying degrees of priority and importance:

First, it is impossible for a European country alone, or even for Western Europe as a whole, to imagine a European Grand Strategy that offers any prospect of success in these regions.

Second, it is obvious that a purely national American strategy, and its implementation by the United States alone, can have only limited success.

Third, success depends in most cases on the prudent use of our economic potential.

Fourth, we can by military means prevent dangers from developing into wars or even into defeat, but we cannot by military means defuse the underlying, dangerous economic situations, which we have to try to understand.

Fifth, the West needs greater understanding of the history and culture, as well as the economic situations and social aspirations, of the nations in other parts of the world. This applies to Israel but also to the Muslim fundamentalism of the Shi'ites and Sunnis in the Middle East. It applies to the religious, economic, and social background of the Spanish- and Portuguese-speaking Latin Americans. It applies to the Chinese, Japanese, and Koreans and their particular historic heritage.

My message is: Do not let us lapse into the same mistake the Europeans made in the nineteenth century and almost up to the middle of the twentieth century, namely, to look at the world from a purely Eurocentric viewpoint. This means now: Do not let us look at the world from a purely American viewpoint, with North America as the center of the world.

The greater the cooperation between North America and Europe, the better the chances are of stabilizing the economies of other countries and thereby maintaining peace. The greater the cooperation between the West as a whole and the developing countries in all the regions I have mentioned, the better the chances of improving their economic performance, their economic and social well-being, and thereby our own.

If, jointly, we can agree on such a Grand Strategy, the possibility of conflict or war will diminish, but it will certainly not completely disappear. Nor will the Russians' insecurity complex or inferiority complex or Grand Strategy of expansion disappear. As in the past, the Soviet Union will try to exploit regional situations, whether in Central America or South America, in the Middle East, or, later on, in the Far East. They will try to sneak in in the hope of being able to exploit the situation later. To contain the Soviet Union, it therefore remains imperative for the West to remain on its guard and maintain a military equilibrium.

But our military effort must not impair our economic capabilities and performance; it must be held down to what we can afford. The best hope for the Western industrialized democracies to hold their ground lies in the economic field. It is the economic field that offers the greatest prospect for the success of the West, not the military field.

4

Economic and
Financial Challenges

The Structural Upheaval in the World Economy

The economic crisis of the world is not just cyclical but is structural. It is a structural crisis in many ways. As I have already pointed out, it is a depression for billions of people. Some say that the world is in an economic upswing. This is simply not true. It was true only of the United States and a very few other countries. It is not true of Europe and certainly not true of Central America or South America or of all of Africa and Asia except for the five East and Southeast Asian states I mentioned in the last chapter.

What started the structural upheaval in the first place was the Vietnam War and the inflationary financing of it. This triggered a number of dollar crises, in the second place, which led to the collapse in March 1973 of the Bretton Woods system of internationally fixed exchange rates. Governments thereby got rid of the obligation to observe exchange-rate discipline in their monetary and fiscal behavior. Without the necessity for each country to keep its own currency at the fixed exchange rate, the dams against inflation disappeared and double-digit inflation started, even in industrialized countries.

Third, in October 1973 and early 1974, during and after the 1973 Middle East war, OPEC, successfully exploiting the world monetary inflation, caused the first oil price shock and in 1979–80 the second oil price shock. Oil had cost about $1.50 per barrel in the early 1970s; it rose to something like $35 a barrel a couple of years ago and today stands around $27. The twentyfold increase in the price of oil between 1973 and 1982 led to an enormous upheaval in the worldwide network of balances of payments, affecting almost every country in the world and making it necessary for many to resort to financing from others.

The war in Vietnam ended in 1975. The 1973 war in the Middle East did not last very long, and the Suez Canal was reopened rather quickly thereafter. As oil prices rose, consumption dropped, cutting the demand for tankers and for steel. This led to a glut in steel-making and shipbuilding capacity all over the world. The recession that began in 1974 then led to a further decline in the demand for steel, for ships, and so on.

In the roller-coaster course of the 1970s—and it remains true today—almost all of the governments in the industrialized world lost sight of what had earlier been called the magic quadrangle of economic goals, namely, high employment as the first cornerstone, stable prices as the second, sufficient growth as the third, and equilibrium with the outside world economy as the fourth. There is no economy right now among the major industrialized economies of the world that is able to meet all four goals to an adequate degree. And I am not even talking about a possible fifth cornerstone, like a socially just distribution of incomes, or a sixth cornerstone, like ecological equilibrium. The crisis has affected almost everyone, including the Soviet Union and its client states.

Let me give you a few figures to illustrate how certain specific industries have been hit. In 1960 the world had a steel-making capacity of 420 million tons a year. At the end of the two wars I mentioned (Vietnam and the Middle East) world steel-making capacity had risen to 835 million tons a year. By 1983, two years ago, the steel-making capacity was 1,000 million tons a year, but only 67 percent was being used. In earlier years—in 1960 or 1970 or just before the first oil shock or at the end of the two wars—83 percent or 85 percent or 86 percent of capacity was being used. Right now, the world is using around 65 percent of its steel-making capacity. In the United States, the percentage of steel-making capacity being used in 1983 was just 56 percent. In Europe, whose steel industry had once been the backbone of industry as a whole, 59 percent of capacity was being used. Even in Japan, only 62 percent of capacity was being used in 1983. The consequences are alike in Pittsburgh and Cleveland, in Sheffield and Luxembourg, and in the Ruhr Valley of Germany.

Now a few figures on shipbuilding, which was a strong pillar in the British economy and also in the Scandinavian and German economies. In 1960, nearly 9 million gross registered tons of ships were being built in shipyards all over the world. At the end of the two wars, in 1975, 35 million gross tons were being built. The demand for new ships has decreased ever since, of course. But the number of available ships multiplied, and the aggregate capacity of sea transport increased threefold from 1960 to the end of the 1970s. During the period of the two wars, all available ships were being used; by 1983, 52 million gross registered tons of ships were unused and in 1984, even after a limited upturn, 35 million. Today, ships are moored by the hundreds and by the tens of millions of registered tons.

Another branch of our economies that went out of control was grain, or agricultural products in general. Ten years ago, for example, the European Community produced 94 percent of the grain it consumed, so that it was a net importer. Today it produces 105 percent of the grain it needs and has become a major force in world grain markets. Meanwhile U.S. grain production and export capacity have likewise increased. There is a grain surplus in the world. Both Europe and the United States have been subsidizing their farmers all this time and have thereby stimulated overproduction—just as they have done by subsidizing steel-making and shipbuilding.

These are simply major and striking examples. They show the degree of upheaval that has characterized this period, not only in balances of payments and not only in exchange rates between the major currencies in the world but also in very important markets of both industrially and agriculturally produced goods. In sum, the changes have altered the basic structures of many national economies and the pattern of world trade.

As a result of the upheavals, all the industrialized states had a severe recession in 1980, 1981, and 1982, with some a little earlier or later than others (Switzerland, for example, in 1982 and 1983). The recession led to low growth rates in all the industrialized countries. At present, European growth rates are at a level of about 2 percent, for instance. (This, by the way, is the figure one should bear in mind to avoid being deluded by the economic upswing in the United States in 1983 and 1984.) World trade also decreased in 1981 and 1982. All the countries that depend heavily on exports have been hurt by the worldwide decrease in demand. The global effect of high real interest rates, originating in the United States, has done the rest. Investment in productive capital has diminished and so have the activities of branches of industries in the West that produce capital goods and equipment.

And the result of all this has been unemployment rates such as the industrialized world has not seen since the 1930s—rates that tend inevitably to destabilize societies politically and socially. Politically, this has meant accelerated pressure for changes in policy, or, failing these, for changes in government. In a country like France, with a left-of-center administration, some people tend to vote for the extreme right, as more than 10 percent of the French did in voting for M. Le Pen in the 1984 French elections for the European Assembly. Or, if the administration is more to the right of center, people tend to vote for the extreme left, as the 7 percent in Germany did who voted for the Greens in the 1983 German national election. The same trend is to be expected in other European countries; it will grow with the growing proportion of long-term unemployed.

Of course, the political response to economic decline takes different forms in nondemocratic states. When the governing military junta in Argentina attempted in 1982 to seize the Falkland/Malvinas Islands, its action (or at least its timing) was in large part designed to capture public attention, divert it from growing economic troubles, and prevent riots in the streets of Buenos Aires. The Solidarity movement in Poland might not have started had it not been for the severe economic pressure on the whole nation, which had lived beyond its means. The withering of Khomeini's popularity in Iran is another illustration of the impact of economic factors. Many more examples might be given, but the point can be summed up in a simple and central conclusion: the longer and deeper the economic depression, the greater the political destabilization all over the world.

The U.S. Deficit as a Time Bomb

I have already analyzed the South American debt crisis, which is a time bomb that continues to tick. It has been partially defused for the time being, but by no means forever and by no means completely.

In the meantime, we have a second time bomb to deal with. President Reagan has rather optimistically spoken of a second American revolution. In view of the extraordinary expansion of the American economy in the last two years and its considerable financing by other nations' money, I am inclined to be somewhat skeptical of Mr. Reagan's economic vision of the future. How much longer can capital flow from other economies into the United States, into New York City? What will happen if the inflow of foreign capital into the United States dries up? Or is even reversed?

Chairman Paul Volcker of the Federal Reserve Board, whom I regard as an outstanding helmsman of monetary policy in the Western world, has again and again voiced strong warnings with respect to American budgetary policies, particularly the deficits, which result in high interest levels and in a dollar exchange rate that remains, as of mid-1985, still well above a reasonable level. Volcker has pointed out quite correctly that, as the United States continues to draw heavily on the world's savings, there is a drag on internally generated expansion in the other economies. He has emphasized repeatedly that the United States is in the process of moving from the world's largest creditor to the world's largest debtor, that there is the danger of a breakdown in the flow of funds on which the United States has depended to satisfy public and private capital needs, and that there are numerous examples of the serious consequences of excessive indebtedness.

I think all this is correct, and I think also that Martin Feldstein, former chairman of the President's Council of Economic Advisers, was correct in stressing many of these same points. Volcker has also been right in saying, over and over, that it is impossible for the central banks of the world to bring down the excessively high dollar exchange rate by means of market interventions. Even if they were to sell all their dollars, they would not only be stripping their currency reserves but, even more important, they would generate severe deflationary pressures on their own currencies and economies.

Volcker is one of the few American economists whose published view is not restricted to the domestic consequences of continued American deficit spending. He is one of the very few who tries to make the American public understand the implications for the world economy. Most of the members of the Reagan administration seem to have a strong tendency to pass over the implications for the world economy (if indeed they recognize them) and to rely on their country's vast political power to handle external economic threats.

The fact that President Reagan actually does not seem to be worried about the enormous trade and current-account deficits being accumulated under his administration would seem to reflect a serene neglect of responsibility toward the world economy. At the same time, the Reagan administration does favor cutting the size of the federal budget deficit, which is good. But the kinds of proposals it has put forward through the first seven months of 1985 still envisage deficits that are predicted to be in the range of $150–250 billion by 1988; the administration bases its predictions on the assumption that the American economy will expand at an annual average rate of 4 percent in real terms. Needless to say, this is an optimistic assumption. It will certainly not be attained this year. And if there should be a recession in the course of the next few years, instead of the sustained growth hoped for, the budget deficit could very well double to $400 billion a year. This figure may not be very likely; before things got this bad circumstances would force Congress to economize or raise taxes. However, it is no less plausible than the figures given by the administration.

In considering the U.S. budget deficit there is an important point that I have found to be little discussed in the American economic debate. Politicians, and even many economists, seem to be easily misled into measuring budget deficits in terms of their percentage of GNP. Using this yardstick, the present and prospective American budget deficits— at 5–6 percent of GNP—hardly compare favorably with the situation in other industrial countries, although they do not look extremely bad either.

A more important measure, however, is the relationship between the size of budget deficits and the size of savings in the individual nation. Savings rates differ markedly among industrialized countries and are notably low in the United States. Only by putting these two figures together can one arrive at a judgment as to how much a particular government will draw on domestic savings to finance its deficits and whether its interest rates will have to be higher than the rates other borrowers would be willing to pay. If the private sector, including business, does not save enough, then not enough savings will be available for the government to draw on. If the government needs to borrow money anyway, either it has to be provided by the central bank, which would have to print money for this purpose, or it has to come from abroad. Countries with low private-sector savings rates thus have less room for maneuver in borrowing than countries in which savings rates are higher.

The United States has the lowest savings rate of all the large industrial countries. In the past two years, around 6 percent of the disposable income of private American households went into savings, and over the years this percentage has been roughly the same. (It actually dropped after the tax cuts that began in 1981.) In comparison, personal savings in Germany currently amount to 11–12 percent of disposable income and in Japan 18 percent or more.

Thus, if one were to assume approximately the same corporate capital requirement levels on a percentage basis in the three economies, the Germans could have permitted themselves a budget deficit, relatively speaking, twice as high as the Americans and the Japanese three times as high, based on the percentage of net savings the deficit represents. In 1982, the Japanese public sector overall drew off just under 25 percent of private savings, in 1983 just under 22 percent, and in 1984 just 20 percent. The figure for 1985 will be smaller. In 1982, 1983, and 1984, the German public sector borrowing requirement amounted to over 40 percent, over 30 percent, and over 20 percent of net savings, respectively. The trend for 1985 is again toward a lower figure.

In sharp contrast, the American public sector in 1982 consumed 70 percent of net savings, in 1983 the same, in 1984 about 50 percent, with a predicted increase for 1985. In other words, given the fact that under Volcker's aegis the Federal Reserve has consistently refused to print money to pay for deficits, all that was left to satisfy the capital requirements of industry, commerce, the building trades, consumers, etc., was the smaller part of domestic savings—certainly not nearly enough for economic recovery.

It has therefore been necessary to import a large volume of capital from abroad. In 1984 this amounted to a net figure of $100 billion, corresponding to the current-account deficit. It is estimated that the volume of capital imports will be even higher in 1985. Thus the American foreign debt is growing rapidly.

The world's most affluent country is in the process of crossing the threshold between net foreign assets and net foreign liabilities. In the winter of 1985–86, the United States will have the world's largest foreign debt, exceeding even that of Brazil. To be sure, the American economy is a great deal larger and more vibrant than Brazil's. Just the same, like Brazil the United States will not receive any net transfers from foreign assets. Instead, it will have to pay out more in interest to foreign lenders and profits to foreign investors than it receives from its own investments abroad.

Under normal circumstances a country can make net transfers abroad only to the extent that it has trade and current-account surpluses. In contrast to Brazil, the United States does not have such surpluses at the moment. It should be attempting to bring about a large increase in its exports of goods and services, it should be throttling imports, and, above all, the dollar exchange rate should be stabilized at a level 20 percent lower than it is now in order to make exported American goods and services cheaper and more competitive again and to make Japanese and European imports, currently cheap because of the overvalued dollar, relatively more expensive.

A downward trend in the value of the dollar was expected when the dollar was at the level of 2.60 deutsche marks early in 1984. Since then it has risen to over DM 3.40 (in March 1985) and then fallen, as of the end of July 1985, to an intermediate position at DM 2.81. But the adjustment, up to that point, had still not gone nearly far enough and the dollar remained, by any reckoning, substantially overvalued.

Let me review the three reasons for the overvaluation of the dollar:

1. The need to finance the large American budget deficit drove interest rates up. Any foreign investor

who invests his savings or undistributed earnings in the United States instead of in his own country gets an unusually high rate of real interest on his investment—a strong incentive.

2. There is a strong demand in the American private capital market. American companies are currently making good profits, enabling them to pay high interest rates and still pay good dividends, while the American consumer is able to deduct from his taxable income the interest paid in financing a new car or a new television set—again, a strong incentive for investment.

3. There are large numbers of people in Japan, the Middle East, Europe, and South America who prefer to keep part of their assets in the United States, since they have confidence in the long-term vitality of the American economy and perceive the United States as a safe haven for their money because of the political stability it offers or because they feel there are too many uncertainties in their own countries.

In all three cases, the investment of foreign capital in the United States leads to the same practical result, that is, anyone who buys American securities, stocks, or real estate has to exchange his yen or marks for dollars on the foreign exchange market. However, since Volcker is not printing additional money, the supply of dollars cannot keep pace. Therefore, the dollar exchange rate continues to be high.

The consequences of American deficit spending so far have been partly positive and partly negative for the rest of the world.

Positive: The American deficit has triggered an enormous boom in the American demand for goods. This has been of as much benefit to the Japanese and European export sectors and, as such, to the employment situation in these countries as it has been to the American economy. In the United States itself, the boom in demand and the pressure of import competition have resulted in exceptional entrepreneurial achievements. At the same time, American labor has contributed to the recovery by showing unexpected mobility and flexibility. The budget deficit has been a driving force for the economy. This success has greatly increased American self-confidence.

Negative: In Europe, South America, and elsewhere in the world, interest rates are too high. On average, the long-term real interest rate (nominal rate minus inflation) in the United States stood in the spring of 1985 at 8.8 percent; in France it was 5.9 percent, in Germany 5.4 percent, and in Britain 5.2 percent. Not enough is being invested in real terms, since in many cases profits that might be expected are lower than interest yields. Demand is low in the capital goods industries and the building sector. Unemployment levels are much too high outside the dollar area.

As of mid-1985—indeed well before then—the negative consequences were starting to overwhelm the positive ones. What will be the outcome? I have already dealt with the dangers for the debtor countries. There is also a growing danger to international trade in general. Around the world the distortion of exchange rates caused by the dollar has led to a growing distortion of international trade. This in turn has provoked high-handed interventions into the markets almost everywhere. Because of thousands of subsidies and protective measures, half of world trade is already outside GATT regulations. However, if the dollar were to fall rapidly, this would result in enormous reversals in international trade and in the employment situation.

The near collapse of the Continental Illinois Bank in Chicago provided a foretaste of another type of danger. It was not possible to restore the confidence of the bank's depositors (some of them foreign) until the American government offered a full guarantee on all deposits. However, there may be times when a government reaction like this may come too late. Other mass psychological triggering factors are imaginable as well. Not long ago a large headline in the *Financial Times* read, "One Day the Bubble Will Burst." Any reasonable person has to hope that this will not happen. Any reasonable government in the world has to help to see that it does not happen. A loss of confidence could lead to a rapid withdrawal of the mostly short-term foreign investments in the United States. In hours or days, one depositor can infect others with his fears.

A massive withdrawal of foreign funds from the United States—in effect a run on the banks, individually and collectively—would not only mean trouble for American banks; it would also cause a rapid decline in the dollar exchange rate. The exchange value of European, Japanese, and Arab dollar investments would decline drastically, and the volume of their foreign assets would fall dramatically. The damage would presumably be uncontrollable and unpredictable. There is the possibility that American interest rates could go up once again because of a shortage of capital. This in turn could trigger a deep recession.

So one would hope for a gradual correction of the situation, effected by a reduction in the budget deficit over two or three years, which would lead to a gradual decline in the dollar exchange rate. There are three ways to reduce the deficit, that is, by increasing revenues, by cutting expenditures, or by a mixture of the two. Higher taxes will be unavoidable if the sum of cuts in the defense budget (which I believe to be immensely inflated) and cuts in civilian programs cannot do the job. In any event, the widely discussed deficit reduction target of $50 billion this year will be effective only if, in addition, a similarly large reduction is made in the deficit next year and again in the third year.

To be sure, a reduction in the deficit would weaken economic demand in the United States and the world; a reduction in demand would lower both the dollar interest rate and dollar exchange rate. Exporters in the rest of the world would suffer as a result, while American exports would grow. However, lower interest rates would help South America bear its interest burden. At the same time, lower interest levels would help Europe create a larger volume of investment-oriented employment. It would then probably be necessary and possible for some European countries—Germany, for example—to expand their budget deficits without endangering themselves.

It is conceivable that the contraction in the world economy that resulted from a reduction in the American budget would be greater than necessary or more than would be economically bearable. However, if Washington chooses not to act at all, the world will suffer even more. The longer it takes for the "budget surgeon" to take up his scalpel, the greater the probability that the operation will be performed too late. It is bad enough that the world monetary system established forty years ago at Bretton Woods has been destroyed as a result of wrong budget policies in many countries. We must not let this process go any further. We are all part of an integrated system.

H *On Economic Summitry*

enry Kissinger said in late 1984 that, because of America's great economic strength, its politicians and the people who elect them feel that the country is relatively independent of world economic trends. He noted that Americans would have to change this way of thinking if they wanted to overcome chronic economic instability in the world. As Kissinger put it, the times and the American potential require that the country take a dramatic lead.

He was right. Those who attend economic summit meetings will have to help the American president see that a time bomb is indeed ticking and help him defuse it before it is too late. Unfortunately this challenge was not met at the 1985 summit meeting in Bonn—and only in part because the economic discussions at that meeting were overshadowed, in public attention, by the controversy over President Reagan's visits to memorial sites in West Germany. Nor has it been met at any of the recent summit meetings.

The first economic summit meeting, held ten years ago in Rambouillet under the chairmanship of Valéry Giscard d'Estaing, was probably the best. A small group, we met in a large living room. None of us was able to talk to television reporters from our own countries, since the press was kept at a distance. Instead, we had to concentrate on our five partners, speaking to them and listening to them. We left Rambouillet with the feeling that we were thus better able to cooperate with one another. The press was not informed until after the meeting, but it had no shortage of things to report.

Today thousands of journalists travel to the summit locations. Every hour the press spokesmen for the various heads of state and government rush the scripts of statements to their respective national presses. The result is that presidents and prime ministers tend to direct what they say in the summit debates to the public at home in California, the Palatinate, or Paris.

I realize that the effectiveness of economic summitry has declined in this decade. Still, summits can be helpful. We do not necessarily need parallel economic policies, but we do need complementary policies. Sheer American optimism will not suffice, although I readily admit that the pessimist is wrong as often as the optimist—though the optimist is much happier. The United States tends to push at the summit meetings for more free trade in the world. The Europeans tend to respond that the chances for a new GATT round are not good as long as the will to bring about more sensible and stable exchange rates and lower interest rates is lacking.

In fact both are right, and 1985 would have been a special opportunity to make progress, since none of the seven participating leaders has had to face an election in this year. Thus the failure to reach any meaningful agreement at Bonn was a setback. If it means that for some time to come the West will still lack the willpower to take the economic fate of the world into its hands, then there will be a further loss in Western cohesion and we shall continue to be far from having a coherent Grand Strategy.

East-West Trade

Finally, let me say a word about a matter on which there remains a serious and lasting difference of views between the United States and the West European nations. The Europeans dislike the American tendency to use trade measures as means of economic warfare. They disliked Jimmy Carter's grain embargo against Moscow, as well as his economic embargo and other sanctions against Iran during the crisis over the seizure of the American Embassy hostages. And they were much more sharply and adversely affected by Ronald Reagan's pipeline embargo against themselves (although it was intended to hurt the Soviet Union). They do not want to embark on a war of economic attrition against Moscow.

Such a war is certainly something the Russians fear. I have no doubt that they are aware of the inferiority of their economic performance as compared to that of the Western world as a whole and the United States in particular. But if the Politburo in the Kremlin tells the nation that Mother Russia is in peril, that the West is out to conquer it economically, and that the people must therefore tighten their belts even more, they will do so. The Russians are the greatest sufferers in the world; sometimes they even have a passion for suffering. One has only to read the great Russian literature of the nineteenth century to understand this. It means that there is no possibility of winning a war of economic attrition against Moscow.

Most of the American trade restrictions that have been imposed and then called off have hurt the European economies more than the Soviet economy. Such strategies cannot be maintained over a long period of time, and the European allies will not agree to them. The Europeans have been trading with the

Russians for centuries. They believe trading with a close neighbor is politically and psychologically a good thing even if the volume of trade is small (Germany's trade with the 265 million people of the Soviet Union is only about half as large as its trade with the 7 million people of Austria, for example). The Europeans have trade agreements with the Soviet Union; the German-Soviet agreement reaches into the next century. They want these agreements to be honored. And they expect the United States to respect treaties concluded by its allies.

Let me conclude this chapter, though, by coming back just once more to the overriding current economic policy problem—the size of the American budget deficit. Governments are like wheelbarrows. They are useful, but they need to be pushed. If Americans understand that their deficit is really bad for the United States and for the rest of the world, they must push their government a little bit. Getting the deficit under control will be a long and uphill task.

5

Consensus

and Leadership

In the last chapter I strongly criticized the current economic policies of the American government. Aside from this specific and, I hope, temporary situation, I have great confidence in America's leadership potential. The American nation has more vitality than any of the other large nations of the world. It is the most generous, when its generosity is called upon. It has the greatest amount of energy to put behind its policies and, on top of that, it has the optimism I mentioned earlier, which sometimes strikes us rather skeptical Europeans as naive or embarrassing but obviously helps Americans.

Right now, the American president has a chance to make a new start in many fields. He has been given an overwhelming mandate. A new start is really needed in some areas, and I think it is possible. From long experience in cooperating with four American presidents, I will make one prediction regarding new initiatives: In the first stage, a long-drawn-out one, the administration and Congress, governors and professors, and the public will haggle and struggle over analysis and purpose; they will also misunderstand each other. The debate will be wild, and no one in Japan or in Europe will understand clearly where it is all leading. The outcome will be difficult for us outsiders to foresee.

But then comes the second stage. All of a sudden, a phase will emerge in which the United States comes up with an idea for a response to the challenges, an idea for a remedy and for improvement—as the United States did in conceiving the United Nations; as it did in conceiving, together with John Maynard Keynes, the International Monetary Fund; as it did in conceiving the Marshall Plan and the North Atlantic Treaty under Truman; as it did in conceiving the Kennedy round in the early 1960s under the General Agreement on Tariffs and Trade; as it did in conceiving the Non-Proliferation Treaty (after a long Multi-Lateral Force debate that was going in the opposite direction); and as it did in conceiving the SALT I and ABM Treaty breakthrough under Nixon.

If these historical precedents are followed, then a third phase will emerge immediately, which is intended to be very short: Washington will ask its friends and allies in the world to please follow suit within the next forty-eight hours. It will be deeply disappointed if the Japanese or the Europeans or the Russians need more time than just a couple of hours or weeks or if they want to accept only part of the American plan and add some other elements to it.

It is true that neither the Europeans nor the Japanese nor any other allies of the United States have given any American president such a mandate. But almost all of us have known for decades that, because of the sheer size of the United States and its economic and military potential, any American president is actually the preeminent leader of the Western world. An American president may be a perfect leader, he may be an adequate leader, he may be a poor leader. This depends on circumstances, on personalities; it also depends on the personalities of those with whom the president must cooperate, those at the helm in allied countries, in friendly countries, or in the Soviet Union. These other helmsmen will be more willing to cooperate with an American president the less their ally in Washington relies on hegemony, or domination, and the less he appears as Big Brother in charge of the entire family.

But America needs the entire family. There are only two geostrategic areas in which the United States might hope to pursue its interests effectively without cooperation from any of its allies. One is the field of mutual intercontinental nuclear threats and counterthreats, otherwise known as strategic deterrence. The other is the geostrategic small area of Central America—the Isthmus land bridge and perhaps parts of the Caribbean Sea.

In a great many geostrategic areas, however, the United States cannot hope to achieve its goals without the willing cooperation of others in the West. This is true of the economic well-being of South America and the prevention of Soviet interference on that continent. The United States alone cannot guarantee peace in South America. It cannot resolve the debt crisis itself.

The same is true of Black Africa. The dangerous racial conflicts in southern Africa, in particular, cannot be settled by the United States alone. Nor can the conflicts in the Middle East, from Cyprus to Pakistan and from Afghanistan to the horn of Africa, and particularly the conflicts between Syria, Lebanon, Egypt, and Jordan, on the one hand, and Israel, on the other.

And the situation is similar in the Far East, although to a lesser extent, because the United States will be able, by itself, to maintain a military equilibrium for some time. But it cannot rescue either Cambodia or Laos, nor can it effectively direct the economic and political development of that region by itself.

Although, next to Canada, the Western European nations are the closest allies and friends the United States has in the world, it cannot control economic and political developments in Canada or Western Europe either. The North Americans cannot hope to defend the other side of the North Atlantic unless the Europeans do most of the job themselves.

As for American Grand Strategy vis-à-vis the Soviet Union, it is not conceivable for the United States to contain the Soviet expansionist thrust in three neighboring continents—Europe, Asia, and Africa—without the strategic cooperation of many other nations on its side who are also concerned by Russian expansionism. On the face of things, given Moscow's almost dictatorial hegemony over most of its client states and allies, the Soviet Union would appear to enjoy more autonomy in its Grand Strategy than the United States. True, the Soviet Union must act within great limitations—economic limitations, for example—even though these are self-imposed. But there is a sharp difference: What the Soviet Union can decide for its alliance, unilaterally and within the Politburo alone, the United States has to achieve by voluntary cooperation among sovereign states—a much more difficult process.

Indeed, this is especially true in the economic field. The United States cannot gain lasting economic prosperity for itself without a great amount of cooperation with at least the other industrialized countries.

To sum up, with only two exceptions, the strategic interests of the United States outside its borders and—as far as its economy is concerned—even partially within its borders cannot be effectively pursued without alliances and without the cooperation of others. The notion of "going it alone," or isolationism, may sometimes be very tempting, but it will lead to failure and loss in areas where the United States has vital interests to defend.

All nations have interests. These differ and in many cases conflict with each other. This is because of different geographic positions, different national sizes, and different degrees of economic development or achievement, as well as different historical and cultural backgrounds and the psychologies and ideologies that have developed as a consequence. The great task for the West is to bring about fair compromises among the differing interests within our family—and to do this again and again, as changing situations require. Only thus can we harmonize different national goals into one common strategy among friends and allies who will at the same time remain competitors in many fields.

There is an even larger group of nations in the world which—although they remain apart and distance themselves from the great power struggle—need to find compromises among themselves and with others, at least with their neighbors. There are many more than a hundred nonaligned or neutral states, which in their own way face similar necessities locally, regionally, or occasionally even on a global basis, as for example over economic issues.

There is perhaps one great power in the world—the People's Republic of China—that can pursue its national interests today without having to rely on cooperation with allies. But this may change in the medium-term future, perhaps in fifteen years. And the statement holds true only if and as long as China's geostrategic interests remain rather limited in scope; if they extend beyond these limits, the Chinese also will not be able to go it alone.

At the start of this discussion I looked at the world from the standpoint of the United States. Now let us look at the same world from a European viewpoint. For the European sovereign states the prospects for pursuing their own national interests are very narrowly limited. Only by close cooperation and joint action can they hope to enjoy satisfactory economic performance. This is true of the United Kingdom as well, even if most of England's political leaders still need a lot more time and more negative experiences to understand and accept this as fact. The major cooperative structure is, of course, the European Economic Community, but even outside that structure countries like Norway, Sweden, Finland, Austria, Switzerland, and Yugoslavia can thrive economically only if they cooperate closely with the EEC and only if the member states of the EEC cooperate closely with each other.

All of the European states are more export- and import-oriented than the United States. All of them need close economic cooperation with the United States and with the industrialized developed countries of the OECD. The necessity for close cooperation among the Western states for their own economic well-being was clearly seen nearly forty years ago; when the Atlantic treaty was drafted, a paragraph was inserted that stated the common purpose of economic cooperation between North America and Europe, in other words, among the member states of the North Atlantic alliance.

The European states cannot for the foreseeable future defend themselves alone against nuclear threats from the Soviet Union. They need their American allies for this. And in order to maintain the credibility in Moscow of the American commitment to the nuclear strategic defense of Europe, the Europeans need an American presence in Europe. But no European government believes that the nuclear danger is the greatest or most imminent danger. In Germany only intellectuals among the Green party seriously believe that nuclear war is Europe's greatest or most imminent threat. Certainly, as I have pointed out earlier, the European governments are not convinced of the advisability of going into the procurement of Star Wars hardware under the Strategic Defense Initiative, although they are reluctant to say so publicly, because they do not want to embarrass the American administration. The general public is concerned that SDI may have unforeseeable consequences, whereas the governments are concerned that it might lead to further neglect of our joint conventional defense posture.

The greatest European fears are pressure from the Russians, blackmail by the Russians (perhaps against individual Western European countries), and a high level of tension between West and East. The European allies certainly have the potential of jointly holding their ground with conventional arms and troops—even with only token American participation—against any Soviet pressure or attempt to influence Western Europe politically or dominate it. They have the potential thereby to deter Moscow from any conventional attack along the lines of Afghanistan or Vietnam or Cambodia. The great deficiency does not lie in the potential of Western Europe. Rather it lies in the fact that one of the two strongest military powers in Europe, namely France, has not made its troops and military manpower reserves available as part of NATO's joint military structure, joint planning, and joint command. If they would do so, which would be in their interest as well as in the interest of the Western Europeans and the Americans, then of course (as I have made clear earlier) the high command post would have to go to a French general, not to an American. The number of American troops on European soil could then be substantially reduced. But at present this is all wishful thinking. At present Europe's defense requires considerable American participation.

With respect to other geostrategic regions in the world, the Europeans have no chance of successfully pursuing their own interests to any meaningful extent except in cooperation with the United States. Only together with the United States can the Europeans keep the sea lanes from the Persian Gulf to Europe open. But since no one in the world can prevent a group of madmen from setting the oilfields on fire, the Europeans have the same interest in the Middle East as the Americans: to maintain equilibrium and to extinguish brush fires as they appear— and they will appear again in that unstable and conflict-laden region of the world.

Taking all this into account, the Europeans depend on the Americans even more than the Americans depend on the Europeans. Both may find relief in the coming change in the world power structure that China's ascent will cause. This will relieve the West of some portion of the Russian threat, but of course it is in our interest and the Chinese interest that we not abandon our watch.

In my view, there is a large degree of congruity in our sets of values in the West: the open society, the democratic structures of our polities; the basic human rights of the individual and his or her individual pursuit of happiness. No significant differences in basic values will show up whether they are defined at Yale or Oxford or in France, Germany, Scandinavia, Italy, or Greece. These values are not understood and are certainly not accepted by communist dictatorships; they are instead endangered by them and by their expansionism.

Therefore we have to contain that expansionism. We have to contain the expansion of Soviet influence all over the world, and we have to be able to deter them from attacking us or individual members of our family by, in the first instance, maintaining sufficient conventional military forces. The only military forces that have practical application are conventional forces.

In the second instance, the West has to deter the East from using nuclear weapons. But I remind you that, whenever even so-called tactical nuclear weapons are used on the central European battlefield, they will kill people by the tens of millions in a day. This would not only destroy what we wanted to defend but would bring an end to the defense of the center of Europe by conventional means. The present American tendency to concentrate its military planning almost exclusively on nuclear war is abhorrent to me. Conventional war is dreadful enough—I was in a conventional war for more than five years. The nuclear emphasis is profoundly wrong as a strategic priority.

At the level of Grand Strategy, our first priority

has to be to keep the alliance together, and this means, among other things, to keep it together economically. The second priority is a joint Grand Strategy vis-à-vis the Soviet Union, which would not be possible if we failed in our first priority. It is my conviction that the joint Grand Strategy on which the alliance agreed at the end of 1967 under the aegis of Pierre Harmel is still valid.

If we adhere to Harmel's double-track philosophy, it is necessary to carry forward three processes in Europe. The first is the Helsinki process, with the continued active participation of the United States and Canada, now being carried on in Helsinki again. The second is the process of further integrating and strengthening West European institutions, the European Economic Community in particular. The third is a process that has come to a standstill in the last couple of years, namely, the process of further integrating the defense of Western Europe, in other words, the process of creating a West European defense identity.

As far as nuclear weapons are concerned, we are living in an era of delicate stalemate. The weapons of each side ensure that the weapons of the other side are not used. Such mutual deterrence is not, in my judgment, either immoral or illogical. It has maintained nuclear peace for a long time in spite of serious East-West crises. But mutual deterrence may not safeguard peace forever, and behind it yawns the atomic holocaust.

Therefore I am deeply interested in limiting the

nuclear risks. I am not asking for the complete elim-
ination of nuclear weapons. But as a first step we
ought to reduce our Western reliance on them. I
would support all those, in the United States too,
who advocate that the Atlantic alliance move toward
a military strategy of "no early use" of such weapons.
A number of conditions would, of course, have to be
met. It would mean improving our capabilities in
conventional warfare through reallocation of available funds and manpower. It would mean organizing
and utilizing more effectively existing military manpower reserves in Western Europe. It would mean a
much greater role for France and French forces.

The Europeans are at least as much interested in
curbing the arms race as the Americans. Controlling
the arms race is strategically and economically necessary. It is necessary also from a moral point of
view. The subject deserves another book, so I will
confine myself here to a few things outside the tech-
nicalities of arms control. Number one: it must be
understood that arms control negotiations mean cooperation with the Soviet Union. Anyone who does
not accept this should not go to a negotiating table,
or he deceives his nation and the people of the world.
To negotiate arms control means to cooperate with
the Russians—whether we like them or hate them.
Number two: it means forgoing the temptation to
launch an arms race in order to engage in an undeclared economic war of attrition. Number three: arms
control negotiations make sense only if the negotiating parties understand that no one of them can

guarantee its own security by itself. If it could do so, it would not need arms control negotiations. Any theoretically possible "absolute security" for one party means insecurity for all the others. And absolute security is imaginable in theory only in seminars, not in the real world. In the real world, arms limitation negotiations need a certain amount of partnership among those who negotiate with or against each other in order to conclude a treaty.

If a treaty is to be ratified afterward—by the Senate in Washington, for example—one has to be able to show that it is balanced, that the other side does not gain more than we gain, and that we do not lose more than they lose. This means that a treaty on arms limitation or arms control can be concluded only if the will to accept equilibrium is present from the outset to the end of the negotiations. It is still a hard job to convince one's own public and parliament that equilibrium is maintained in a particular treaty—whether it is SALT I, ABM, SALT II, or whatever. That is one of the reasons why there has been so little progress in ratified treaties in the last twelve or more years; given the rhetoric they had been using, governments were unable to convince their parliaments and publics that the results of their negotiations were just and fair treaties.

In order to engage in cooperative negotiations, it is necessary to refrain from mutual abuse and insult. What is needed instead is confidence building on both sides. I think there may be more than a 50 percent probability right now that, within the next three years, the two superpowers may get some initial, partial results in their negotiations in Geneva. But then there should be a parallel normalization of relations in a number of economic fields and trade and even in cultural exchanges. I would underline and emphasize what the Aspen International Group recently stated: Containing and influencing Soviet power requires that the West be strong and cohesive and consistent. But it does not require confrontation; instead it requires sustained engagement.

A cohesive joint Grand Strategy has to have many facets and components. By no means does it consist only of a military posture or only of procurement of hardware or only of arms limitation negotiations. It is general diplomacy as well. The procurement of hardware has almost nothing to do with diplomacy; it is necessary, but it is not a substitute for a strategy that is lacking. A cohesive Grand Strategy for the West includes economic policy inside our own camp as well as vis-à-vis the Soviet Union and a coherent economic policy toward the developing countries in the Third World that occupy those disputed or endangered geostrategic regions I dealt with to some extent in chapter 3.

Leadership in Short Supply

The current lack of a coherent strategy in the Western world is based on man-made circumstances. It is based above all on an absence of leadership. This applies to both Europe and the United States. Since the establishment of the European Monetary System and the election of the European Parliament in Strasbourg, there has been no more genuine progress in Europe. Because of a lack of inner cohesion, Europe is currently incapable of action or leadership in any of the many different areas of activity I have discussed in this book.

The size of the United States, its vitality and dynamic energy, the fact that it has a genuine common market (rather than one in name only) consisting of 235 million people, with a single currency and a single legal and tax system, and, finally, its superior military strength mean that, given the state of the Western world in the mid-1980s, the leadership role can be assumed only by the United States. However, the United States is not prepared to lead. Instead, isolationist, America-centered, hegemonial, and internationalist tendencies vie for supremacy.

This need not continue to be the case. Leadership emanated from Harry Truman, George Marshall, and Dean Acheson. It was reflected in Eisenhower's pragmatism, Kennedy's vision, and Nixon's outstanding ability to assess strategic situations and make the corresponding decisions. I do not doubt that this can be so again in the future. In free countries with democratic constitutions, leadership must reflect both strength of conception and the will and ability to engage in compromise and arrive at a consensus.

Consensus is possible. As I have already pointed out, despite all the differences in our histories and our cultures, we all act on the basis of what are, in principle, the same fundamental values. We all believe that the dignity of the human individual must be inviolable. We are all convinced of the need for an open society and for the rule of law. We all desire justice, solidarity, and peace among nations. And we are all aware of our responsibility. Our governments can do justice to their responsibility only by acting, not by adopting tactical communiqués formulated to appeal to public opinion in their own countries.

6

A Best-Case Scenario

Among the governments and publics of the West today, worst-case scenarios reign supreme; we spend inordinate time and thought on the worst that can happen, which not only diverts our attention from the possibility of positive action but often turns our minds to extreme and unrealistic approaches. Worst-case psychoses can be found in places as diverse as the peace movement, Soviet propaganda, and Ronald Reagan. The latter's Star Wars initiative, for example, is an attempted response to an obsession with a worst case affecting his own nation, that is, the case of an intercontinental nuclear missile attack on the United States. It is still not clear whether and under what circumstances Reagan's Strategic Defense Initiative will be able to contribute to the overall security of the world. What is clear, however, is that it cannot contribute to the economic and social welfare of the nations of the world. In other words, it is at best a partial response. At best...

It is time the Western nations did some joint thinking on how to respond to more than just a small part of all conceivable cases, that is, more than just a (highly improbable!) worst case. It is time we engaged in joint thinking on how we can enable the world as a whole to move toward a conceivable best case on the basis of joint efforts, making use of all the intellectual, diplomatic, economic, and military potentials and instruments at our disposal.

If the world is to be kept in overall economic, social, and military equilibrium, the West needs internal cohesion in its European, North American, and Japanese alliance. It needs joint strategies not only against Soviet expansionism but also for the welfare of the developing countries in the Third World. Finally, the West needs a coherent concept of its own economic development. None of the elements necessary for this is inconceivable. None need conflict with other elements.

Since the second half of the 1970s, the degree of consensus has been declining. It is time for government leaders to concentrate once again on the essential. Drawing on my many years of experience, I would like in this final chapter to frame a comprehensive set of propositions—some already set forth, a few covering points for which there was not space in earlier chapters. Together, I believe these propositions would represent—if they could be adopted and acted on—a best-case scenario for a Western Grand Strategy.

1

On the Alliance

We renew the two-track philosophy of the North Atlantic Council Resolution of December 1967, the way to which was paved by John F. Kennedy, Pierre Harmel, and others. We continue to support both "main functions" of the Atlantic alliance:

a. "to maintain adequate military strength and political solidarity to deter aggression and other forms of pressure and to defend the territory of member countries if aggression should occur."

b. "to pursue the search for progress towards a more stable relationship" with the Soviet Union and the Warsaw Pact countries.

2. At the same time, we renew Kennedy's concept of solidarity based on an American and a European pillar. We recognize the need for a third pillar in Japan. None of us will undertake major steps in the external security sector without previously consulting our allies.

3. We invite France to reorganize its armed forces, particularly its conventional forces and reserves, for forward defense purposes in Europe. This should take place together with other Western European armed forces and under the supreme command of a French officer.

4 On the Soviet Union

We do not strive for superiority. Instead we want a stable balance of military forces in Europe.

5. To this end, we will change the structure and equipment of our armed forces in Europe, so that any decision on the actual first use of nuclear weapons

will not have to be made by us. Instead, in the future we want to shift the first-use decision to the Soviet Union.

6. At the same time, we pursue the establishment of a stable security balance on the basis of negotiations and treaties aimed at arms limitations in five areas:

    a. conventional forces in Europe;

    b. nuclear weapons, including INF, in Europe;

    c. strategic nuclear weapons;

    d. space-based weapons;

    e. confidence-building agreements in all of the above-mentioned areas. We will not, however, enter into any agreements compliance with which we cannot verify or monitor by our own means.

7

On the Third World

We accept and respect genuine nonalignment of any country that adopts this policy.

8. We will provide economic aid to help create acceptable economic conditions in the Third World that will make a life in dignity possible. We will do this both for moral reasons and to prevent Soviet exploitation of degrading living conditions and intervention. We will thus continue, and strengthen, official development aid, in spite of continued nonparticipation by the Soviet Union.

9. At the same time, we appeal to the countries of the Third World:

a. to undertake a substantial cutback in military spending, which today amounts to many times the amount of development aid received;

b. to open up their economies to direct investment by foreign companies, thus making possible a broad transfer of both technology and productive capital.

10. We will not hinder birth control policies in the developing countries and will support every ethically conscionable approach to family planning, so that population explosions can be avoided which would predictably trigger economic crises that could not be brought under control.

11. We jointly offer the Central American states a Reagan Plan, à la George Marshall, to help them establish viable economies that would double per capita GNP levels within seven years.

12. At the same time, we shall work, initially through our finance ministers, to formulate a proposal aimed at defusing the time bomb contained in the debt crisis. In this context we assume that the debtor and creditor countries, as well as the OPEC states, bear a common responsibility for the situation that followed the two oil price shocks. We are willing to negotiate a General Agreement to Lend, which would include debt rescheduling that would delay repayment for many years and provide predictability of annual transfers.

13

On Our Own Economic Problems

In the near future we will take the following mutually supplementary steps:

a. The United States will reduce its structural budget deficit for fiscal 1986 by about $50 billion and for fiscal 1987 by about another $50 billion and, in addition, provide tax incentives for private-sector savings in an attempt to lower market interest rates and the dollar exchange rate;

b. The European countries will at the same time expand their internal demand spending, primarily in the form of tax reductions, in order to compensate partially for the predictable drop in American demand and counter a further rise in unemployment;

c. Japan will take similar steps; in addition, in view of the low level of Japan's defense expenditures in past decades (and the same trend will continue in the future), it will rapidly expand its development aid program and in this way help to reduce the Japanese balance-of-payments surplus.

14. We commit ourselves from this day on not to introduce any kind of additional export subsidy or import hindrance or any other kind of additional protectionist measure.

15. We will jointly support a new GATT round. In the "Reagan round," we expect negotiations to go on for several years.

16. At the same time, at the individual level, we

will initiate a process with regard to our national financial and economic policies that will, in the long run, lead to more stable exchange rates among our currencies. We have come to recognize that the excessive exchange rate fluctuations of the past twelve years—never before seen in the world economy—were the main cause of distortions in international price structures and international competition, as well as of the growth of protectionism. We know that more stable exchange rates on the foreign exchange money markets cannot be imposed by central bank interventions today. What is needed instead is an overall system of national economic policies aimed at achieving and maintaining current-accounts equilibria. For this reason, we consider an international monetary conference desirable prior to the conclusion of a GATT round.

17. Independent of this, the European countries will strengthen the role of the European Monetary System and the écu. The North American countries and Japan expect that, over the medium term, the possibility will emerge of establishing fairly stable exchange rates between the dollar, the yen, and the écu—something toward which they wish to contribute. All of the participating states are aware that, if this objective is not attained, new monetary-based distortions in the prices of internationally traded goods will necessarily result in a new danger to the system of free world trade.

18. We jointly recognize that, after we have overcome the current crises and dislocations, it will be

necessary for all of the economies in the advanced industrial countries to act in the world economy as net capital exporters, for the benefit not only of the Third World but also of themselves.

19

On the Ecological Problems of the World

From the Sahel to the tropical forests, from the whale populations to the forests of Central Europe, from the increasing change in the earth's atmosphere to the declining quality of ground water, we recognize numerous dangers to our natural environment. They cannot be sufficiently curbed at the national level alone. For this reason we support a joint scientific survey and investigation of the causes and mutual dependencies involved. We would like to initiate this effort in a United Nations context. Involvement of all nations will be necessary, regardless of their political systems, their alliance or non-alliance status, and the stage they have reached in their development.

Of course I know that the leaders of the Western world are not prepared for an agenda of this kind today. They would probably not be able to agree on a single one of the nineteen points I have listed. The list could be varied greatly. It would be possible to limit it to just a few items, or other important items could be added.

At the first summit meetings in the 1970s, we did not deal with comprehensive lists of formulated objectives. However, we conducted talks with each other that were actually as comprehensive as this. In the 1980s this is unfortunately no longer the case. The heads of state and government of the Western world have to be urged to look beyond the issues of the day to the important, essential issues.

None of the nineteen proposals I have listed above is utopian. Is it wishful thinking to hope that the heads of government can deal with such a comprehensive package?

Harmel Report & strategy:

———————————

pp. 11-14. 3rd phase of Western postwar
p. 143 - "still valid"   "grand strategy